The Osier Cage

ROBERT O. EVANS

The
Osier Cage

Rhetorical Devices in
Romeo & Juliet

UNIVERSITY OF KENTUCKY PRESS
LEXINGTON, 1966

To my wife

Acknowledgments

MUCH OF WHAT I have to say finds support in the insights
of the many critics to whom I acknowledge my great in-
debtedness. Some of them are cited in the documentation,
but it is indeed difficult to single out a special few to whom I
owe the most. I have found there is something to learn from
almost all of them, even those with whom I find myself in
most violent disagreement. Criticism is an organic process
despite the belief of some writers that they have had the
final word. Even the Coleridges and the Bradleys must
inevitably be revised by later generations.

I am indebted to the Research Fund of the University of
Kentucky for material assistance in the preparation of this
study. In a very different sense I am indebted to Professor
Ants Oras who first called my attention to the whole method
of approach.

ROBERT O. EVANS
Lexington, Kentucky

Contents

Introduction

THIS ESSAY WORKS towards an interpretation of *Romeo and Juliet* from a limited point of view. It is an exegesis of Shakespeare's rhetoric, particularly his use of certain of the tropes and figures of speech so familiar to writers in the Renaissance but so often concealed from us. Nevertheless, even minute analysis should adhere to certain general principles. Inherent in the whole following methodology is the assumption that *Romeo and Juliet* is best considered as drama, not as pure poetry, though it is essentially the rhetorical splendor of the poetry that will be examined.

One chapter investigates some of the important speeches of Romeo and Juliet and defines the controlling devices Shakespeare wove into them. The figure highly characteristic of the language of both hero and heroine is *oxymoron*; nowhere in literature are there to be found extended passages of *oxymora* to equal those Shakespeare wrote for Romeo and Juliet. Then follows an examination, again in terms of rhetoric, of the role of Friar Laurence in the play. Friar Laurence serves as a catalyst between the warring houses of Montague and Capulet and also between the lovers and the outer world of Verona. This role is very different from the one he played in Arthur Broke's poem, Shakespeare's direct source. The function of the friar in the play has been signally neglected by the commentators.

There follows an examination of a more particular problem —the relation of Mercutio's famous Queen Mab speech to the structure of the tragedy as a whole. The reader will discover that I do not consider the Queen Mab speech a delightful digression; rather I see it as an important part of the whole fabric of the play. Again the point of departure is the rhetorical figure, which leads inevitably to a larger vision.

Because of this concern with diction it may surprise the reader to discover that my interpretation and methodology are, in a sense, quite Aristotelian. I see *Romeo and Juliet* not as a breathtaking jewel among love stories but rather as a reasonably well integrated drama to which all of the parts, including the devices of diction, make a contribution. I find no important digressions. To support that impression I first undertook a study of the Queen Mab speech. I find that Shakespeare's structure is tight and his plot satisfactory. I am not disturbed that Romeo did not simply spirit Juliet away to Mantua after he was exiled, though that would have been the easiest physical solution to the problem that confronted the lovers. That was not the play Shakespeare wrote. To us the actions in the plot seem more reasonable than the characters from which they arise, but I am not convinced an Elizabethan audience saw the play that way. To the Elizabethans characterization must have been clearer than it is for us, partly because they understood the rhetorical devices Shakespeare used to delineate his subjects.

No attempt is made here to analyze all of the devices of diction in the play. That would entail a different methodology. On the contrary, only a few devices are examined— those which lend themselves to the solution of certain problems. Indeed, in all of Shakespeare's plays the devices themselves are not especially interesting, except perhaps to the rhetorician. Rather, the way Shakespeare used some of them to further his development of plot and character (those two elements which, according to Aristotle, are the most important aspects of any tragedy) is important. Only as clues to meaning do I justify examination of the figures at all. As Shakespeare himself reminds us, the play's the thing.

Perhaps the single statement repeated most frequently about *Romeo and Juliet* is that it is a very lyrical play. Few would dispute this. It begins with a sonnet, contains arias and duets, and may be spoken of in operatic terms. The great French literary historian, Taine, called the conversations of the lovers *"les roulades des rossignols,"* and I can think of no better statement of the lyrical quality of their lines. But the play is also highly rhetorical. Unfortunately that statement made in the present century, when lyricism and rhetoric are often considered to reside in opposing camps, has a derogatory ring. There is hardly a passage in the play devoid of rhetorical devices, and very little has been said by commentators about what these devices are or why Shakespeare chose to employ them. I have not made any attempt to tabulate the figures of rhetoric, for this, in a summary fashion, has already been done and the results reported in an article by J. W. Draper, "Patterns of Style in *Romeo and Juliet*," in *Studia Neophilologica* (XXI, 1948-49). Doubtless a new tabulation would reach somewhat different results, for Shakespeare's use of devices is so complex that any count is bound to reflect many matters that depend on the interpretation of the tabulator. There is no reason to believe that a quantitative analysis of the figures would serve more than our academic interests. Shakespeare could write in a highly rhetorical fashion or in a plain unornamented style. To count the figures would tell us what we already know, which of these moods was upon him in this play or that.

Later, I trust, it will become clearer just how difficult it is to isolate the figures that appear in *Romeo and Juliet*, and even if we were able to do this beyond dispute we should still not know how Shakespeare named these devices. There might also be some merit in examining the figures that occur most frequently, but at present, without more knowledge than we have of Shakespeare's opinions about the hierarchy of rhetorical devices, we might find ourselves over-emphasizing certain figures of a very simple nature that occur repeatedly throughout the poetry without having very much special dramatic significance. Unfortunately we cannot look directly into the Renaissance rhetoric books for an explanation of Shakespeare's schemes because, in the first place, the writers who deal extensively with the figures attempt to explain everything in those terms. Moreover, they are singularly reticent about value judgments. At one end of the spectrum Renaissance rhetoricians spoke of ordinary alliteration as a figure of rhetoric; at the other end they sometimes mention allegory. Neither of these is a rhetorical figure in our sense of the term and alliteration, particularly, occurs everywhere in Shakespeare. I have no doubt he thought of it much as we do—as a matter of prosody.

With perhaps pardonable enthusiasm the figurist critics wished to include in their schemes nearly everything that came to their attention. They approached the subject with the eye of a surgeon and the assumptions of an Aristotelian (even when they were noted Ramists), never with the ear of a poet or the eye of a theatre-goer. The whole, however they went about examining it, was the sum of its parts, and as diction was that part in which they were particularly interested, they divided it into as many parts as possible. Accordingly, they treated as figures many matters that we, and Shakespeare, too, would have considered something quite different. For instance, among the subjects that the Ramist Abraham Fraunce included in his *Arcadian Rhetorike* were rhyme and stanza form. But there is no reason to assume that

Shakespeare thought the same way, though it is safe to assume that he had read many of the works on rhetoric. A careful examination of the plays suggests that Shakespeare's ideas about how the figures should be used were probably formed through practice in the schoolroom, not by a study of inclusive schemes. As Richard Sherry says in his *Schemes and Tropes* (1550), "The common scholemasters be wont in readynge, to saye vnto their scholers: *Hic est figura*: and sometyme to axe them, *Per quam figura?*" Surely, on many occasions the next question must have been, "*Cur? Quapropter?*" Or, in our terms, what is the function of this figure in that particular context in the *Amores* or the *Aeneid?* In this fashion Shakespeare must have formed some very sophisticated ideas about when and why to use devices to secure particular dramatic effects, and the practice he employed in *Romeo and Juliet* provides a summary of nearly all he learned.

Most interesting about Shakespeare's rhetoric is a small number of devices, quite separate from prosodic matters, that he used in an absolutely startling fashion to emphasize dramatic structure. Writers of the rhetorics, who usually based their examples on Latin literature, would have been astonished had they carefully examined Shakespeare's texts. It is his brilliant, incendiary use of figures that captures our imaginations and causes us to ask again and again why he did exactly what he did at a particular point in the drama. But his devices are not merely functional; I am sure he intended to arouse admiration for the performance. Sidney had added to pity and fear—the Aristotelian aims of tragedy— the Renaissance conception of admiration, and Shakespeare interpreted it to include admiration for technical brilliance. The essays which follow attempt to cast some light on these matters so important for our understanding of Shakespeare's diction, his mastery of words.

Nevertheless, each of the chapters except the one dealing

with *oxymora* discusses devices that are readily recognizable from Renaissance rhetoric books, especially those of the figurists, Angel Day, Henry Peacham, George Puttenham, and Richard Sherry. In these works, which are seldom read by modern students of Shakespeare, *oxymoron* somehow escapes scrutiny, but it was a device well known in antiquity and certainly understood by Shakespeare and his contemporaries. Shakespeare must have met it often in the schoolroom, where his education was largely in Latin. Any lingering doubts we may have entertained on that score were long ago dispelled by T. W. Baldwin's monumental study, *William Shakspere's Small Latine & Lesse Greeke.*

Not only is each essay an *explication de texte* of certain rhetorical figures, but it is also an explication of devices that would have been readily recognized by Shakespeare's audience even at the speed lines are delivered from a stage. To the Elizabethan ear many of the figures that we must work out laboriously were neither particularly delicate nor difficult to recognize, though Shakespeare brought to their usage an entirely new complexity. Our education is such that we have lost the ability to hear the figures of rhetoric and sometimes even to see them on a printed page, though their effects on our interpretation of meaning have very likely not entirely disappeared. To Shakespeare and his audience such devices were, first, part of the ornamentation of the play, but Shakespeare often used them in a far bolder fashion to lead his audience to conceptions useful for understanding his meaning. They are, above everything else, devices of economy, permitting the poet to move quickly from one subject to another without bothering to supply full documentation of either plot or character that might otherwise clutter the play.

But Shakespeare seldom relied on any single device to make a point. He was a popular dramatist whose success depended on his being understood by the theatre audience. His method is the antithesis of that of a writer like Henry James, who liked to weave delicate, subtle symbols into the fabric of his novels to reveal to the astute reader a pattern in the carpet. That method would be wasted in drama where the clues are oral and come very quickly, and besides it was not to Shakespeare's taste. A good thing, he may have concluded, is worth saying again, and he could not afford to allow anyone to miss it. We often find him telling the same joke again to make sure that even the most thick-skulled clod in the pit got the point. There is a fine example of this technique in *Romeo and Juliet* when the nurse tells the story of her husband's remark to Juliet after the child had fallen on her face and scraped her forehead. "Thou wilt fall backward," the husband said, "when thou hast more wit." As a bawdy Elizabethan remark this one is hardly worth making once, but Shakespeare apparently wished it to emphasize the passionate side of Juliet's nature that the audience would soon see. Juliet had just reached the age for love. Accordingly, he permitted the nurse to tell the joke three times.

My interpretation of the play reflects what I think Shakespeare must have written for his contemporary audience and what that audience may reasonably have been expected to understand. But this is much trickier to decide than it may at first seem, for we are not Elizabethans, and no amount of scholarship can recreate their minds in ours. We do now have a great deal of information about their language, that Coleridge, for instance, did not have, but we have only the sketchiest ideas about their habits of thought. We do not really know the composition of the theatre audience, though we think that Shakespeare himself divided it into two kinds of playgoers, the despised groundlings "capable of nothing but inexplicable dumb shows and noise" and what we assume must have been a more educated, genteel faction. At least a good many commentators seem to share Hamlet's opinion,

but we cannot be certain that, in this matter, Hamlet spoke
for Shakespeare. We ought not to forget that Hamlet had
his own reasons for castigating the groundlings at that point in
the play. His remarks were very quickly to be followed by a
real dumb show on stage that Hamlet had not bargained for—
the mysterious preface to the Mousetrap play that almost
sprung the trap prematurely.

There are other reasons for supposing that Shakespeare
played primarily for an audience with much the same education as his own. The very intimacy of the Elizabethan theatre
required an audience participation quite unknown to persons
accustomed to the proscenium arch. To us the stage is a
picture, and no amount of experimentation with theatre in
the round can dispel our preconceptions formed by scores of
performances. But Shakespeare's audience was as ignorant of
our passive type of reaction as they were of our plush, padded
seats or our subtle lighting effects. Their part in the dramatic
experience was much more active than ours. Even the simple
problem of calming down the audience at the beginning of a
performance, which we accomplish so easily by dimming the
house lights and drawing back the curtain, was a serious
obstacle for the Elizabethan dramatist. And the matter is
even more complicated. The theatre for which Shakespeare
wrote in his youth was surely much less sophisticated about
dramatic conventions than the one he addressed later. The
people who came to see *Romeo and Juliet* were much closer
to the days when the only entertainment along the Bankside
was bear baiting and cock fighting than those who came to see
Antony and Cleopatra. There are experts who have said,
perhaps somewhat metaphorically, that Shakespeare trained
his audience across the boards. Whether that opinion could
be substantiated or not, it is true that the English drama grew
to maturity in his lifetime and that Shakespeare was a major
fashioner of its growth. To some extent my interpretation of

the play must depend on such assumptions, one especially: that by the time of *Romeo and Juliet* (perhaps more so by the time of *Antony and Cleopatra*) a substantial portion of the audience had undergone an education similar to that described by Baldwin.

Unfortunately we have no sociological records of the Elizabethan audience; we can only surmise from the evidence of the plays what they must have been. Even the few hints we think we have, such as stage directions, are not very helpful; besides most of the stage directions were added after Malone. But of one thing we can be reasonably certain. At least a portion of the audience understood the tropes and figures when they heard them; otherwise they would not appear in such abundance in the plays. And to hear them, one had to pay attention to what was happening on stage. Moreover, they found in them a peculiar delight that somehow escapes us. For one thing they loved ornament for its own sake, and the figures were something separate from plot, character, and spectacle for them to applaud. Nevertheless, Shakespeare's business was drama, and he seldom provided pure window-dressing; he made the figures work to further the development of plot and character.

Only the most skeptical modernist needs to be convinced that Shakespeare was a great user of rhetoric, even in the sense that Sir Philip Sidney deplored when he recommended against the use of new-found tropes and strange similes by poets "that do dictionary's methods bring into your rhymes." The late J. Q. Adams, considering this matter in his *Life of Shakespeare* (in 1925), concluded from the evidence of the plays that Shakespeare may have taught for a time in a grammar school in those lost years before he emerged as a poet in London. Sister Miriam Joseph, in *Shakespeare and the Arts of Language*, illustrates from the plays about 200 figures described in Renaissance rhetoric books, many of them with multiple examples. Her method has been to define the figure and then find examples in Shakespeare. That is a valid way of settling certain questions, particularly of indicating, without actually tabulating occurrences (which I believe would be fruitless), the extent to which Shakespeare employed Renaissance rhetoric. But she is not very much concerned with why Shakespeare used a particular figure in a certain context. That is the question here, and it presupposes a different methodology. One first decides on the passage to be examined or, if the problem involves a series of cruxes, the passages. Then it must be ascertained whether or not figures are used and if so how they operate and to what end.

Many difficulties attend this method. An encyclopedia would be required to examine every figure that appears in Shakespeare, but of course there is no need for this. It is also very difficult to classify some of the devices. Permit me to illustrate that problem by a passage from *Romeo and Juliet* that is to be discussed more fully later. "Why railest thou on thy *birth, the heaven and earth?* / Since *birth and heaven and earth*, all three do meet / In thee at once . . ." (III.iii. 119-121, italics mine). To mention the least important matter first, there is a repetition constructed around the substantives *birth, heaven*, and *earth*, repeated in the same order but with a slight change of connectives. In the second occurrence *and* appears for *the* before *heaven*. This may seem a petty consideration, but change of connective was a proper subject of Renaissance rhetoric. Are we, then, in the first phrase dealing with a deliberately omitted conjunction (thus, *asyndeton*), or, as seems more likely, are we in the second dealing with a deliberately added conjunction *(polysyndeton)*? If one were making a statistical tabulation of the figures, that kind of consideration would be very important. What Shakespeare's audience would have noticed, if the lines were properly said by the actors, would be the alteration itself, whether or not they could supply a name to it. And who can say how Shakespeare called the figure? He did not write a book of rhetoric.

Whether we are dealing with *asyndeton* or *polysyndeton* may be a superficial question, for there is another, more important figure bound up in the repetition. The end of one clause occurs again, in substantially the same form, at the beginning of the next (separated only by the connective *since*); this matter could hardly escape the ear of an educated Elizabethan theatre-goer. The figure is *anastrophe*, though— just to complicate matters—there is a reasonably good chance Shakespeare might have called it *epanastrophe*. The distinction is blurred in the rhetorics. Did Shakespeare think, then, that he was constructing a figure within a figure, *asyndeton* within *anastrophe*, perhaps one of those new-found tropes that did not receive notice in the dictionaries? We simply cannot be sure. But there are hundreds of such figures within figures in Shakespeare, far more, I think, than one is likely to find in classical authors.

There is still another figure bound up in the passage cited, though its nature will not be clear out of context. The passage is upbraiding in its tone, and chiding speech was considered by Renaissance rhetoricians to be a figure, *onedismus*. But, wait, the modern student would be likely to complain. That is not the same thing! You are mixing matters of structure with those of feeling! One deals with words, the other with mood. But the rhetoricians themselves brought about this confusion, and probably Shakespeare would have thought as they did if our assumptions about his education are correct. We have no traditional name for these matters that involve a mingling of several figures; therefore, for want of a better terminology, I have called them rhetorical complexes. Such complexes are a special mark of Shakespeare's style in a very rhetorical play like *Romeo and Juliet*—especially when we

compare him with many of his contemporaries. When Shakespeare turned his attention to devices, he brought to their
usage such a wealth of variety that textbook examples, culled
from the writers of antiquity, seem pale beside his.

The rhetoricians considered many of the devices purely
ornamental. Though we often sneer at decoration for its own
sake, there is nothing wrong with considering the figures of
rhetoric in that way. Art is artifice, no matter what the
fashion in which it is wrought. But the Elizabethans found
in the devices a peculiar delight that is largely foreign to us.
We are not quite sure why, and rhetoricians are mostly silent
about the subject. It seems that ornamentation concerned
the devices of words rather than mood. It is hard to see how
chiding speech (*onedismus*), for example, could be ornamental
and not functional, for it is dictated by the intention of the
passage. Certain kinds of plain speech, too, were considered
to be rhetorical. *Julius Caesar* is a play in the plain style
(excepting perhaps Antony's funeral oration) with few verbal
ornaments compared to *Romeo and Juliet*. But the stoic
restraint we descry in the speeches of Brutus is an example
of rhetoric in functional operation. It delineates character.
The style of *Romeo and Juliet*, certainly highly ornamented, is
equally functional. We look upon all adornment, except that
attached to the female body, as undesirable and forget that it
may serve a purpose, though in *Romeo and Juliet* the reason
may sometimes be obscured by the lyrical qualities of the
play. Thus, to some commentators, a play is debased because
of its ornamentation.

We seem unaware that a case for admiring the ornamentation in a play like *Romeo and Juliet* may be constructed without reference to the functional use of devices in terms of the
Platonic psychology widely held at the time. The doctrine
of the tripartite soul, divided into appetite, will, and reason
(sometimes called body, will, and wit) presumed speech to

be the special attribute of man, connected with the rational portion of the soul. As rhetoric is a highly developed aspect of speech, it follows that an exquisite use of figures indicated high development of wit or reason. Renaissance rhetoricians do not make the point quite that way, but they would not find it incompatible. Such an interpretation partly explains why the Renaissance held rhetoric in such high esteem, though tradition, too, supported that opinion. It is unfair and inaccurate of us to assume that the Humanists handed the laurel over to pedants, though the scholars were often pedantic enough. Instead, they gave way before the new psychology.

Romeo and Juliet is a very witty play. In the first two acts a high percentage of Romeo's lines are devoted to wit, especially the kind we should call repartee. Romeo's role begins with a word game in which he tries to score points against Benvolio, and later Mercutio, and virtually everything Romeo says up to the ball at the Capulets is part of the game. Even when he meets Juliet, they are playing word games, though not of course the same ones. That is not to say that Romeo's speeches prior to the ball are digressive or do not constitute a very important function in the play. But it is important not to forget that they are also passages of high rhetorical wit. There is a sound dramatic reason for this beyond sheer entertainment; neither Romeo nor Juliet are, in an Aristotelian sense, very appropriate subjects for tragedy. They might do well enough in a *Mirror for Magistrates*, but as new tragedy for the Elizabethan stage they involved grave risks.

We cannot be certain that Shakespeare knew Aristotle even through the many commentators, or for that matter Minturno or Scaliger, or even Sidney (though the last seems almost beyond dispute), but we can say that what they knew about the drama he had also learned in the hard school of practical theatre. He knew it would be dangerous to slay two sweet, attractive young people. He understood from writing his histories, if nothing else, how important it was for tragic heroes to be better than average men. Whether he could have verbalized about the proper emotions to be aroused by tragedy, pity and fear and admiration, as Sidney could, is beside the point. He realized that one of his tasks as a dramatist was to supply both Romeo and Juliet with attributes of character that would elevate them to tragic status. Failure to do so would have resulted in a very different sort of play. Considering the position Romeo and Juliet held in the society of Verona he selected for his milieu, one thinks of the risk involved as one of descending unintentionally to domestic tragedy. Thus, he made Romeo, and particularly Juliet, the wittiest people in an especially witty play, which is not far from saying he made them the most rational. But he did not allow the matter to rest there—on wit alone. Particularly with Juliet, who presented the more serious difficulty, being female and only fourteen, he carefully provided a comparison between her and the sun in the heavens. "And Juliet is the sun," Romeo tells us. By the doctrine of correspondence the sun was equated with the head, the seat of reason. Then Shakespeare constructed in both Romeo and Juliet a tension between passion and reason, almost a paradox that the most rational beings in the play are also the most passionate, from which his tragedy could arise. He was turning Aristotle's doctrine of tragic flaw into a complex psychological analysis. Moreover, the Elizabethan audience, trained from childhood on rhetoric, would have recognized most of the clues he furnished. To us the play probably remains more of a mystery than Shakespeare intended (at least reading the commentaries seems to indicate so), and we are not quite sure when the play is over why we have experienced emotions proper to tragedy.

It may seem easy for Shakespeare to have equated wit with

reason (a century later it would have been much more difficult) and to have used that means to raise his hero and
heroine to tragic stature. But working against that contention,
at least superficially, would be the inordinate amount of false
wit we find in Shakespeare, especially in the mouths of
servants. False wit, however, does not detract from the high
value placed on genuine wit—proceeding from reason, that
part of the soul nearest to God in the divine scheme. Men
of the Renaissance would have distinguished one from the
other. Besides, rhetoric books are also filled with false examples alongside the true ones. There, devices are often
paralleled by their inversions. A good syllogism may be placed
beside a false one so that the scholar could learn to distinguish
one from the other. But wherever he found it, that Shakespeare learned the lesson well is evident in the plays. And he
did not confine false wit to the lower classes either; compare
the funeral oration of Brutus with that of Antony to see how
deliberate was Shakespeare's practice. Moreover, he seldom
overemphasizes the false side, though it was part of the fun
to permit the servants sometimes to get the better of their
masters in the game of repartee. Shakespeare must have loved
the whole business, for he experimented with many aspects of
it. In *King Lear*, for instance, he tried a very heavy amount
of sound reason in the mouth of the fool, though he was also
playing with a favorite theme of appearance and reality. But
most of the time, I think, the audience understood what he
was doing and savored it.

We need not labor the question here, for it is clear even
to the modern reader, who does not understand many of the
devices with which Shakespeare furnished clues to the Elizabethan audience, that Romeo and Juliet are the true wits of
the play. But Shakespeare rarely relied on rhetorical devices
alone to make a point; he let imagery, verse, action all tell the
same story—until it is hard to miss the point. That was his

method. We do not need to understand the doctrine of
correspondence to know that Juliet described as the sun is an
elevating conceit. Part of what we call the universality of
Shakespeare is simply his habit of laboring a dramatically
important point in many ways. Surely proof of the sureness
of this unsubtle technique is the lasting popularity of the
plays.

Many of the devices with which Shakespeare made clear
his dramatic intentions were figures of rhetoric. While it is
not necessary to understand them all, or even sometimes to
recognize them to follow the main developments of plot and
character, they were the clues to meaning that he furnished
with great care for his own audience. Indeed, he extended
so much care to the devices that we are persuaded that the
Elizabethans must have understood how they worked. Also,
there are some places in the play, some matters, where the
meaning is especially dependent on the rhetorical figures,
though these are almost never places of high importance in
the action. For example, Mercutio's famous Queen Mab
speech seems to be related to the dramatic action almost
entirely through its figures. That we have often missed this
relationship is witnessed by the many commentators who
consider the speech digressive. For understanding the meaning of the play, I contend, an understanding of the figures is
desirable even when not absolutely necessary. An attempt to
remind present day readers of some of the tropes and figures
of rhetoric, in their most ambitious sense is an attempt to
revive a lost skill. Each chapter deals with a very separate and
different aspect of the play. These matters may sometimes
seem peripheral, but it will be seen that they do support a
reasonably consistent interpretation of the play presented in
the final chapter. This interpretation is neither especially
revolutionary nor wholly original. It is not my claim that the
critics and commentators have reached wrong or misleading

interpretations of *Romeo and Juliet*. Quite the contrary—most of my interpretation, the reader will quickly recognize, is reflected in the many statements about the play already made by Shakespeare scholars. But that the rhetoric of the play adds support to certain views, and makes some interpretations seem more desirable than others, has hitherto gone largely unremarked.

CHAPTER TWO

Oxymoron
As Key To Structure

We find often, in Shakespeare, that a phrase holds all the future, a new universe, while the speaker [or, for that matter, the audience] thinks it is but an idle dropping of words, as apparently meaningless as the heavy drops of rain that come before the thunder, or the little wind that is heard before an earthquake.[1]

IF ANYTHING SEEMS clear to us from a study of Shakespeare's dramatic method, we see that he was a careful weaver of strands to make whole and unique the fabric of his plays. Even Ben Jonson, who was probably responsible for the conception of Shakespeare as the "natural" genius as opposed to the deliberate artist, though he might ask some reservations, would have to concur. "Yet must I not give Nature all," he wrote, "Thy Art, / My gentle Shakespeare must enjoy a part" ("Upon Master William Shakespeare," prefatory to the 1640 edition of the *Poems*).

Most of the threads in the dramas first appear near the beginning, for Shakespeare was accustomed to supply us at once with what is necessary for the action and to proceed from there, adding little (except of course in the chronicle plays) that does not follow from what was originally given. The beginning of *Romeo and Juliet* is leisurely; there are fifty lines spoken between Sampson and Gregory and then with

Abraham and Balthasar, servants of the Capulets and Montagues respectively, before Benvolio comes on stage to part the fools (who are about to quarrel) and start the action. Those fifty lines are necessary, for they introduce us to the violence of the feud between the families (though the sonnet prologue had already brought up the matter), and they also introduce us to the sensuality that will serve on one side of the contrast between Romeo's love for his unseen mistress, Rosaline, and his pure, true passion for Juliet. In the forthright bawdiness of their speech the servants also prepare us for the entrance of Mercutio, who will pick up the flavor of their words when Shakespeare dispenses with the rude mechanicals. And rude mechanicals they are, for not only are they akin to those he called by that name in *A Midsummer Night's Dream* but they serve also as mechanical devices for getting the play started. Shakespeare had no curtain,[2] no lights, no set stage, no telephone to ring, no aproned maid with a feather duster to answer it saying that madam would come anon.

Yet despite the leisure of fifty or more lines the pace of the servants' conversation is anything but relaxed. They begin with a homonymic pun on *collier-choler-collar*, primarily calculated to call the audience to attention. The play is *Romeo and Juliet*, and its words are important. The pun itself must have been trite, perhaps even exasperatingly so, or Shakespeare would not have used it with no preparation whatsoever (though he seems to have liked it well enough; at least he used it again in *I Henry IV*).[3] From this device, *paronomasia* (sometimes called *agnominatio*),[4] Shakespeare moved easily enough into a form of fallacious reasoning quite appropriate for servants. The passage reads:

Sampson: I strike quickly, being moved.
Gregory: But thou art not quickly moved to strike.
Sampson: A dog of the house of Montague moves me.

Gregory: To move is to stir, and to be valiant is to stand. Therefore, if thou art moved, thou runn'st away.

In the first two lines above there is a neat *chiasmus* (a figure
in which there is marking with diagonals) constructed around
the words *strike quickly* and *quickly . . . strike.* Usually I take
the ability to construct figures, in Shakespeare, to be a sign of
wit and thereby a mark of intellectual power (or reason), but
not infrequently Shakespeare inverts matters and permits the
servants to exhibit the wit, sometimes even at the expense of
their betters. In this case he seems to be offering us a false
scent, for as we follow the reasoning we find we are actually
dealing with another rhetorical device, a form of false reasoning. The mechanism is syllogistic, though there is a term
missing between "to stir" and "runn'st away," but it is doubt-
ful that Shakespeare thought of the passage as a false *enthymeme.* As Sister Miriam Joseph points out, "Renaissance
rhetoricians defined the figure *enthymeme* as a reason given
to things contrary,"[5] thereby considerably altering the meaning of the term from that we commonly understand. Yet there
is a contrary sense involved here; the opposites *to move* and
to stand are wrenched into juxtaposition within the first ten
lines of the play. Doubtless the device encouraged Shakespeare's audience to be attentive; otherwise they might miss
what the play was all about. Then, Shakespeare drew the
parts of the contradiction together in a single line, spoken by
Sampson: "A dog of that house shall *move me to stand*"
(italics mine). He continues, altering the subject quite logi-
cally, to begin the bawdiness, "I will take the wall of any man
or maid of Montague's." As often happens in Shakespeare,
the false wit displayed in this passage is really very witty.

The phrase "move me to stand" is most unusual, for while
on the surface it is deliberately foolish it is also, in terms of
what the servants are saying, very appropriate. Moreover, it

gives Sampson a temporary edge in the word game they have been playing, and it must have been the game itself, as well as the individual pawns, that delighted Shakespeare's audience. But the *oxymoron*-like effect of the phrase "move me to stand" will hardly escape even the modern reader (or listener) unfamiliar with the tropes and figures of rhetoric. Shakespeare has written a pyrotechnical introduction for the bawdiness that is to follow. He has demanded that the audience stop fidgeting and pay attention to what he has to say. And he has, as a passing gesture, characterized the Capulet servants as masters of false wit.

Did he do more? The *oxymoron*-like statement that sums the situation up is very significant to the development of the play. For one thing, this rhetorical display is a bit too prominent to be sheer fireworks. Shakespeare does not let up on us; he keeps reminding us of the drawing together of contrary elements to seem pointedly foolish, and that is a definition of the figure *oxymoron*. For example, Shakespeare reaches for the same effect a few lines later, when the Prince says, "Cankered with peace, to part your cankered hate" (I.i.89). The actual device is slightly altered, but peace and hate (peace and war) are both prefaced with the same word *cankered* (though not the same part of speech), the effect again being to draw together contrary things.

Were we to consider *oxymoron* and *oxymoron*-like effects as they appear in the mouths of characters in the play, we should find that Shakespeare first gives them to the servants and then to the Prince, both agents but neither real characters in the drama. In this arrangement there is a neat, almost rhetorical, sense of balance. After the balance is secured, he passes these devices on to Romeo himself. He is prepared to continue the method with a principal character. A few lines later Romeo speaks his astonishing passage containing more than ten *oxymora*.

Romeo comes on stage, where the servants have recently been brawling, to begin a discussion of love with Benvolio. Then he notices what has happened there (doubtless some of the props, perhaps swords, have been left lying about). He says:

> Here's much to do with hate, but more with love.
> Why, then, O brawling love, O loving hate!
> O anything, of nothing first create!
> O heavy lightness! Serious vanity!
> Mis-shapen chaos of well seeming forms!
> Feather of lead, bright smoke, cold fire, sick health!
> Still-waking sleep, that is not what it is!
> This love I feel, that feel no love in this.
>   (I.i.169-176)

For half a dozen lines Shakespeare has Romeo averaging two *oxymora* per line. I should like to call such passages *extended oxymoron*. The process of extending a trope or a figure seems to have been considered highly desirable in the Renaissance. We are all familiar, for example, with Donne's famous conceit of the "stiff, twin compasses," used to supply unity to the entire poem "A Valediction Forbidding Mourning." The theory seems to have been that the more meaning that could be packed in (even cryptically, if the style is *conceptism*) the better the figure, the more the art. Even allegory, for instance, which Abraham Fraunce discussed under the heading of tropes in his *Arcadian Rhetorike*, was thought of as a "long or continued metaphor."[6]

There is an air of extended metaphor about Romeo's astonishing passage of *oxymora*, for he uses it to draw together the themes of love and war with which he is concerned at the moment, or perhaps we should say there is a further, implied *oxymoron* contained in the extended figure, one dealing with the main subjects of the play itself. The entire

performance is startling, though when we examine the individual *oxymora* themselves they seem, oddly enough, rather
commonplace. It seems as if Romeo were reciting a list of
schoolboy examples: "feather of lead," "bright smoke," "cold
fire," etc. If he were recalling his textbooks, and that would
by no means be beyond the reach of Shakespeare's art,
then two important faculties of the reasonable soul—wit and
memory—as the Elizabethans conceived of it, would be called
in account by the passage. For example, in *The Anatomy of
Melancholy* Burton lists the faculties of the reasonable soul,
calling them "actions": apprehension, composition, division,
discoursing, reasoning, and memory.[7] What I have called wit
was equivalent in Burton's time, and certainly for a long time
before that, to what Burton called "reasoning." Thus the last
two faculties, and perhaps certain of the others as well, are
illustrated by Romeo's speech.

These faculties are called into account to shed light on
Romeo's character, and Shakespeare does the job most eco-
nomically within a few lines of Romeo's entrance on stage.
We see immediately a strong intellectual strain in Romeo
which will develop in two directions, as wit and as lyricism.
Over and over again Shakespeare will show us that Romeo is
the master of most of the other characters at wit, excepting
only Juliet, and virtually every critic has noticed what a fine
poet he can be. This is *Romeo and Juliet*, not *Cyrano de
Bergerac*; nevertheless, the devices in this speech do seem quite
ordinary, perhaps because Romeo is being only partially
qualified at this early stage of the play for his role as tragic
hero. The play begins as comedy, and one of the triumphs of
Romeo and Juliet is that it is, though almost of mixed genre,
successful as a tragedy. Polonius would probably have called
it *comico-tragical*. Considering the nature of the play Shakespeare wisely did not choose to state his entire case at once.
Moreover, at this moment Romeo is wracked by his sensual

passion for Rosaline. He has a long way to travel before he becomes a proper tragic hero. Only after he meets Juliet and ceases to participate in the game of love and courtship, substituting for it real love and grand passion, will his character ascend to match hers.

It may seem that such an interpretation is reading beyond what is given in the play, but the only positive explanation Shakespeare offers us to distinguish Romeo's true passion for Juliet from his sensual attraction for Rosaline is that the former is requited. That statement, made somewhat later to Friar Laurence, may shock some modern readers, but it is true. How can Shakespeare, we may ask, make such an important distinction on such thin grounds? But no matter what we think of it, he did. That distinction is the key to the entire relationship at the beginning. Shakespeare's interpretation of grand passion required reciprocation (here as in *Antony and Cleopatra*). It seems as if Shakespeare were scoffing at the game of pursuit so often played between men and women, and reflected in the sonnet sequences, and offering instead a more exalted vision of sexual relations.

But at this early point in the play it was enough for him to show Romeo as a master of wit, and the *oxymora* accomplish that purpose. Moreover, Romeo has another function in the play at this scene, for his job is to pull together the disparate themes of the play, the themes of love and war (or violence), for the play must eventually turn into tragedy. To anyone who did not know the story, who had not read Broke's poem, the prefatory sonnet would have made that clear. Early in the play most of the words have been comic or directed to the violent side of the contrary. It is finally time, Shakespeare seems to have decided, to remind us that the play is going to be about more than that. I do not think Romeo does a very efficient job of it, for to inform the audience of the direction the play would take could have been better done with plain language. But Shakespeare would try to kill two birds with the same stone. He wanted to show Romeo developing his rhetorical powers; the time would come for him to show us his poetic gifts.

As we might expect, some critics have noted that Romeo is here highly rhetorical and have claimed that this was his mood while he was in love with Rosaline. He changed and became poetic, they seem to think, after he met Juliet. But that is not the way the play develops. Actually Romeo is rhetorical throughout wherever there is need for him to be, and his powers seem to grow at least up to and through the balcony scene. In the Renaissance there was no reason why rhetoric and poetry should not make good bedfellows; in fact they were inseparable. Shakespeare seems to have thought this, for in *Antony and Cleopatra* he added the poetic side to a character, Antony, who was already a master rhetorician (in *Julius Caesar*).[8]

Having exhibited his mental agility and wrenched together the themes of the play in his first speech to Benvolio, Romeo did not abandon the device of *oxymoron*. His second speech turns to the subject of love, at that time his love for Rosaline, ending with this description:

> Love is a smoke made with a fume of sighs;
> Being purged, a fire sparkling in lovers' eyes;
> Being vexed, a sea nourished with lovers' tears.
> What is it else? A madness most discreet,
> A choking gall and a preserving sweet.
> (I.i.184-188)

Here the *oxymoron*-like effect of the last line is reached through *anaphora* (beginning a series of clauses with the same word), and perhaps there is not really a clear-cut example of *oxymoron* at all. That would not have disturbed a Renaissance writer; he would have considered it a part of the art.

"The excellencie of tropes," wrote Fraunce, and there is no reason to think he did not mean all figures and devices, "is then most apparent, when either manie be fitlie included in one word, or one so continued in manie."[9] The result is the same; love is a "choking gall" and a "preserving sweet." The contrary is not constructed in the usual fashion with modifier and substantive of disparate meanings, but the comparison is paradoxical. Love is *bittersweet*. For the moment Romeo has put the signs of violence out of mind and turned to one of the themes of the play, that of love, and only one aspect of love at that, unrequited love as shown by his attraction for Rosaline. The other kind, the grand passion he is soon to feel for Juliet, has yet to be developed in the play, but there is some reason to believe Shakespeare would have seen that, too, as bittersweet. That kind of love was finally to lead to the tragic ending.

There is still another idea but lightly cloaked in these passages, one that may partly serve to distinguish the two kinds of love and make Romeo's seemingly fickle conduct more palatable to the audience. That is the reference to the theme of appearance and reality Shakespeare makes when he speaks of "still-waking sleep, that is not what it is," which is mirrored in the next speech by "madness most discreet." This theme is ubiquitous in the Renaissance. A little later, for example, Calderon was to state it even more forcefully in *La Vida Es Sueno*, where he says that life is a dream and even the dream itself may be a dream.[10] Shakespeare reminds us that appearance is not reality, a lesson Romeo must quickly learn.

We may also be reminded here of the Platonic ladder of love, where man first sees and loves a beautiful woman and then progresses, by orderly steps, to the love of beauty itself. If Shakespeare had that concept in mind, and it is one with which he was certainly familiar, then he has foreshortened

and altered it here. Rosaline may represent the initial step
and Juliet the final, but if that is true, Juliet serves in the play
both as character and symbol. The abbreviation of the
Platonic doctrine, set forth by Ficino and reflected by
Castiglione and many others, would not itself be unusual,
and Shakespeare might have found a model, if he needed one,
in Spenser's *Fowre Hymns*. But the point here is that Shakespeare took a good deal of care to distinguish between the
two kinds of love experienced by Romeo. Without any direct
explanation he managed to persuade the audience that the
attraction for Rosaline was the appearance of love and that
for Juliet the reality. He was being subtly philosophical and
extremely clever in an artistic sense. It was a first step in the
construction of his idea of grand passion on which so much
in *Romeo and Juliet* depends. And the method was essentially
rhetorical.

He continues to associate Romeo with *oxymoron*, among
other things indicating the many-sided tensions in his personality, up to the meeting with Juliet. For instance, as the
revellers are making their way to the Capulet feast as unin-
vited guests, Romeo informs them that he will not dance.
"Being but heavy," he says, "I will bear the light." Again,
the effect is the same. Moreover, that line also lends itself to
interpretation on many levels. Romeo is heavy because he
has been experiencing the choking gall of unrequited love;
soon he will meet Juliet and find the true light, or to maintain
the contrary, the sweet aspect. Light, it has often been noted,
is the central symbol of the play, and Shakespeare proceeds
from this slight, tenuous suggestion of the symbol to his great
crescendo: "But soft! what light through yonder window
breaks? / It is the east, and Juliet is the sun."

Also, one might say, Romeo is heavy as he approaches the
house of the Capulets because he has been chained in the cave
able only to perceive the appearance of love, though he has

some inkling of what may follow. When he sees Juliet, he will know the reality. It is impossible to say whether or not a Platonic allusion at this point is deliberate,[11] but it would be quite unnecessary to recognize where the theme of appearance and reality came from to appreciate its usefulness to the development of Romeo's character—and from that of the plot of the drama. The proof of that is in the play, for we do not accuse Romeo of frivolity, though that is certainly what his actions suggest and what, of course, Friar Laurence, who has not been party to the same development, believes.

If Shakespeare were a simple poet, *oxymoron* as a device might well disappear from the play after the feast. Shakespeare used it to introduce the characterization of Romeo and to point out the contrary nature of the themes of the play. After he had done that, he might have dropped the device, but he does not. Before tracing it further, perhaps I should point out that this figure used so extensively at the beginning of *Romeo and Juliet*—which dominates the rhetoric of the play —is one that is not mentioned in the English rhetoric books of the time.[12] No one knows why *oxymoron* is omitted from consideration, unless because of all the devices of rhetoric it is the easiest to recognize. It was, of course, well known in classical antiquity, though even then rhetoricians were likely to pass over it (notably *Rhetorica ad C. Herennium*).[13] In the two hundred and more figures treated by Sister Miriam Joseph it is also conspicuously absent, because her list was constructed from those in the figurist books. Warren Taylor did not include it in his tabulation of *Tudor Figures of Rhetoric*,[14] after an examination of Charles Butler, Angel Day, Dudley Fenner, Abraham Fraunce, John Hoskins, Henry Peacham, George Puttenham, Richard Rainolde, Richard Sherry, and Thomas Wilson, the most noted rhetoricians that have survived to us. Not all of them, of course, are figurists, and certainly Shakespeare had not read them all; Day's list of figures, for example, appeared only in the 1599 edition of *The English Secretarie.* Clearly Shakespeare did not learn about *oxymora* from them, but he might have from one Latin (or Greek) grammar or another, or, what seems more likely, he might have picked up his knowledge orally in the school-room.[15] Doubtless the boys were asked to add to the examples given them some of their own; that is what "cold fire" and "sick health" sound like. Of all the devices *oxymoron* is one of the easiest to descry and to make, and Shakespeare was the master of at least two hundred figures. Why then should he rely so heavily on the simplest of all in the beginning of *Romeo and Juliet?*

A simple explanation occurs when we think about his audience. Here is a figure even the despised groundlings could hardly misunderstand. If they gave him a fraction of their attention, they were bound to hear the *oxymora* and, the dramatist might be permitted to hope, get the point. But whether this reason occurred to Shakespeare or not we shall never know. In any case he was never again to employ the device quite so frequently or in exactly the same way. And the groundlings must not have changed greatly throughout his career (though some critics believe that Shakespeare gradually succeeded in training his audience). Are we to assume, then, that the device failed, or that he discovered a better method of doing the same thing, or that he simply grew tired of it, or perhaps that its extensive use in *Romeo and Juliet* reflects some peculiar problem of that play?

There may be some truth in all these suggestions, but I think the last is probably the most important. Shakespeare was never again to encounter the same problems in a play, and accordingly he did not need to rely again so heavily on this particular figure. The problem he set for his challenge in *Romeo and Juliet* was not primarily rhetorical at all. It was a problem of theme and character sometimes symbolized by

him in astrological terms. It concerned the conjunction of
two planets, Venus and Mars. As they cross and portend
doom, so the themes of love and war cross and recross in the
play. Indeed, as so many of the critics have noted, one of the
key terms of the play is "star-crossed." But it has far too often
been assumed that by that phrase in the prefatory sonnet,
and what follows from it in the play, Shakespeare meant the
audience to believe the tragedy was inevitable. Romeo slew
Tybalt without meaning him any harm at all. A letter from
Friar Laurence to Romeo explaining the sleeping potion went
astray. Thus some critics have seen Romeo and Juliet as
hapless children, victims rather than tragic hero and heroine.

Perhaps the play is not entirely successful. Shakespeare left
some ambiguity about the ending, and the final victory of love
over death that he seems to imply is unfortunately revealed
to many of us primarily by the pair of golden statues raised to
commemorate the lovers by their respective families. This
victory of love over death is not entirely brought about by
what they manage to say or do, though there are some hints
of what Shakespeare intends in phrases like Juliet's, "Then
I'll be brief. O happy dagger!" (V.iii.168). Perhaps it would
have been clearer if Shakespeare had furnished Romeo and
Juliet with a final dialogue in the tomb instead of permitting
each to soliloquize, but to have done so would have meant to
allow Romeo to speak with Juliet after he was already poi-
soned and dying. Perhaps that would be more than the
audience could bear. For Romeo no alternative existed after
he had slain Paris and entered the monument. From that
instant the ending was inevitable. But despite the ambiguity
of the ending, I believe Shakespeare intended tragedy to arise
from the characters he so carefully constructed, though he was
not working according to any preconceived tragic fashion.
After all, the play began with the intention of being different.
It required two heroes. Nearly half of it might as well have

been comedy as tragedy. It was an experiment with mixed genre, and not any mixture hitherto examined by the commentators. But experiment or not it was calculated somehow to lead to the proper emotions of tragedy, to pity and fear, and admiration, as Sir Philip Sidney had recommended.

To demonstrate that *Romeo and Juliet* does successfully arouse the emotions proper to tragedy might lead us a long way from a demonstration having to do with the figures of rhetoric. But perhaps one further point should be mentioned here to add to the contention that the tragedy arises mainly from character. Shakespeare deliberately altered Juliet's age from sixteen years, as she appeared in his source, Arthur Broke's poem *The Tragical History of Romeus and Juliet* (1562), to fourteen years in the play. Why should he have bothered to change her age unless he needed her to be fourteen in the kind of tragedy he was writing? It might of course be argued that he read Broke carelessly, or even that he thought fourteen an appropriate marriageable age for the Italian setting he was using. But such arguments, which presuppose that the change in Juliet's age was either unintentional or unimportant, do not seem very persuasive in the light of the excessive attention paid to the matter in the play. For the tragedy as he conceived it Shakespeare needed a young girl just on the threshold of sexual awakening. He did not feel he could chance it with a sixteen year old. He needed a Juliet, if he were to arouse the proper emotions, who could not possibly have had any previous romantic experiences, or she could not be the Juliet who has captured our hearts. If the tragedy arose by accident, would it have mattered? In practice Shakespeare usually followed his sources rather closely unless there were sound reasons for deviating from them.

And if the tragedy arises primarily from the careful though unusual characterization, there may be an additional explanation for the heavy play of *oxymora* at the beginning. It seems hard to believe Shakespeare would have relied so heavily on that device, no matter how useful it proved for getting the play started, if the tragedy were to proceed entirely from accident, for *oxymora* take the most deliberate sort of attention in their construction. The device is pointedly foolish (that is its definition); if it were not very deliberate it would just be foolish. What the author is doing with this device is presenting a paradox, and that is what the play is, too. In a real sense the structure of the play is mirrored in Shakespeare's choice of *oxymoron* as his dominant rhetorical device. The macrocosm (in this case the play) is mirrored in the microcosm (the dominant rhetorical figure). Shakespeare extended, it would seem, the doctrine of correspondence into the very rhetoric of the lines.

The author is finally responsible for any figure, but so, in another sense, is the character who utters it. And figures are never a matter of chance; in literature they are always a matter of deliberate artistry. One who creates them in life may conceivably do so by accident and in the next instant be struck down by a thunderbolt. But a play is never quite life, and there the maker of figures does so deliberately. In this play the key figure is *oxymoron*, and Romeo and Juliet are masters of that device. Mercutio, who is marked for death midway through the play, is also a masterful rhetorician, but the figures with which he is specially skillful are not the key figures of the play. *Anaphora* is one. *Chiasmus* is another ("and as soon moved to be moody, and as soon moody to be moved," III.i.12-13). *Zeugma* is still another, and certainly brevity of diction, laconism, is characteristic of Mercutio's speech. (*Zeugma* is a kind of *brachylogy*, usually where two substantives are attached to the same verb, e.g., I eat fat sheep and good wine.) Also *paronomasia* (pun): "Tut, *dun*'s the mouse, the constable's own word. / If thou art *Dun*, we'll draw thee from the mire" (I.iv.40-41). These last, *zeugma*

and *paronomasia,* are figures of obscurity, and there are reasons to believe Shakespeare did not wholeheartedly approve
of obscurity (though he seems to have exempted *paronomasia*).
Possibly he has made Mercutio so much of a *conceptist* in his
speech in order to make him readily dispensable from the
play.[16]

Other characters, too, often show rhetorical ability, sometimes most unlikely ones. Even Lady Capulet is given an
outstanding example of *anastrophe* in a moment of heightened
emotion; "But one, poor one, one poor and loving child"
(IV.v.46).[17] But the great rhetoricians of the play are Romeo
and Juliet, and that is highly appropriate, for in their rhetorical
displays the great themes of the play cross and recross, and
resolution is attained. Mere rhetorical ability is not enough
to assure importance in the play, but a certain rhetorical skill
does provide a sort of guarantee. The whole idea is difficult
for us to understand, uneducated about rhetoric as we are.
But Shakespeare's audience was better prepared than ourselves. Even so, Shakespeare did not leave very much to
chance. To draw attention to the fact that Romeo and Juliet
are the real master rhetoricians of the play and the most
astute manipulators of its main device, *oxymoron,* he once
even permitted Mercutio to parody them: "A very tall man,
a very good blade, a very *good whore!*: (II.iii.27-28, italics
mine).

Unfortunately we cannot say that one figure arouses a
certain emotion and another a different one. The tropes and
figures do not work that way. Renaissance rhetoricians do not
tell us that certain figures serve best in particular situations;
their rhetoric is not so cut and dried. About the most we find
in their works are descriptions of figures that heighten or
amplify. The real decisions are left to the artists; Shakespeare
must attach particular significance to the figures he uses to
define the meaning of the play. In a sense, he must provide

the reality beneath the appearance, and, as we have seen, the figure *oxymoron* is closely connected from the very beginning of *Romeo and Juliet* to the question of appearance and reality. But after Romeo reminds us of this connection on his way to the Capulet feast, that figure recedes from the play for a time, giving way to other means of expression. Then in the balcony scene there is renewed emphasis on the theme of appearance and reality. That scene, however, comes in the second act; before that Romeo and Juliet must meet and play a pretty word game that leads to the exchange of kisses. Doubtless those kisses had a great deal to do with their discovery of true love, but the game that led to them was also important. It helped place Romeo and Juliet on a par of wit. True, Juliet is only fourteen, and she cannot be a day older, but she must also be made into a proper match for her lover, who has more experience of the world and at least one previous love affair. Shakespeare had no intention of violating the gospel of degree in the play, not even intellectually; the lovers must be equally paired. And he was an inveterate feminist. The plays frequently suggest it, and I think they must reflect his personal opinion of women, but the dramatic action of *Romeo and Juliet* requires a feminist point of view. What Shakespeare had hitherto been suggesting by an inference that could be drawn from his easy-to-recognize figures he was now to repeat in a duet between two very witty young people whose concerns revolve around appearance and reality. "What's in a name?" he was to ask when he came to the balcony scene. Indeed, only the appearance is in Montague, which belongs to the outer world of Verona. The reality is human love, grand passion which, sufficiently exalted, may conquer all, even death.

A high point in the play has been reached, and Shakespeare has turned to methods other than rhetorical, but he had not abandoned *oxymoron*. He had already demonstrated Juliet's

intellectual qualities in a charming fashion, so well that she
almost seems superior to her lover. But he had not yet shown
her to be Romeo's equal at his own game. That had to wait
for another high point in the action, when Juliet learned that
her husband had slain her favorite cousin, Tybalt. The nurse
brings that information to her and for the second time fore-
stalls her mistress, nearly driving her to distraction but in no
way diminishing her intellectual powers.

> Hath Romeo slain himself? Say thou but 'I,'
> And that bare vowel 'I' shall poison more
> Than the death-darting eye of cockatrice.
> I am not I, if there be such an I,
> Or those eyes shut, that makes thee answer 'I.'
> If he be slain say 'I,' or if not 'no.'
> Brief sounds determine of my weal and woe.
>   (III.ii.45-51)

The most striking device here is *paronomasia* ('I' in lines 45
and 49 is a misspelling for 'aye': Shakespeare's puns were never
orthographic).[18] The pun *aye-eye-I*, as Juliet makes it, is one
of the cleverest and most serious in Shakespeare, and it may
foreshadow more of the tragedy that follows than first appears.
But it particularly shows us Juliet's intellect sharpened, rather
than blunted, by extreme emotion. The passage ends with
a line that is almost aphoristic in its tone, the figure is
apothegm or *sentence* (or at least resembles that), but so
well blended into Juliet's speech that we are not tempted to
compare her rhetorical methods with those of the friar, whose
speech is characteristically filled with aphorisms. The entire
passage, unusual as it is, prepares the way for an even more
striking one that follows as soon as Juliet learns the truth from
the nurse:

> O God, did Romeo's hand shed Tybalt's blood?
> .   .   .   .

O serpent heart, hid with a flow'ring face!
Did ever dragon keep so fair a cave?
Beautiful tyrant! fiend angelical!
Dove-feathered raven! wolvish-ravening lamb!
Despised substance of divinest show!
Just opposite to what thou justly seem'st,
A damned saint, an honorable villain!

(III.ii.73-79)

Here Juliet treats us to a subtle and extensive complex of figures (e.g. transposition of the position of the modifier, *beautiful tyrant, fiend angelical,* perhaps derived from *enallage:* a very delicate *chiasmus, just opposite to what thou justly* . . . ; etc.) woven around six *oxymora,* all of which are fresh, original figures, not schoolbookish examples. Under the stress of great emotion Juliet becomes a masterful rhetorician. So much for all opinions that plead excessive rhetoric indicates a cheapening of emotional quality. These devices do not lower Juliet in our eyes, nor are they merely verbal tricks for casting her character. They serve to refine her intellect and make her a fitting equal for Romeo (if they do not make her his superior), and they call attention squarely back to the question of appearance and reality on which so much of the play is based. Verona seems one thing but is another. Romeo seems the ideal lover, but "Was ever book containing such vile matter / So fairly bound?" The world which was made for love is actually filled with violence, and a young girl must discover it and search alone, for she has but one night left with Romeo, for resolution.

Though the final tragedy and, perhaps, ensuing victory are still concealed, Juliet begins to find resolution, in terms of her commitment to grand passion, from the moment she begins to seek a rationalization for Tybalt's death at Romeo's hands. "My husband lives that Tybalt would have slain; / And Tybalt's dead that would have slain my husband. / All this is comfort." It is also a neat *chiasmus* and sound reasoning, too. It is the best that Juliet or Shakespeare can do, and perhaps the best that anyone could do in this life without direct recourse to a religious answer. For Juliet, so far as she can tell, there is love left, and one must make the best of what life offers. And then she remembers that Romeo is banished—that dreadful word *banished*. Without Romeo's presence how can she find resolution in love? Death, she fears, not Romeo, must take her maidenhead. As it turns out, it is only a moment of charming, female weakness. She is wrong. Romeo does come that night, but death was not long in following.

It is difficult to describe exactly Juliet's rational processes in terms of Renaissance rhetoric, though there is a sort of *enthymeme* involved in the *chiasmus*. She is, of course, disputing with herself under conditions of grave mental stress. The handbooks do not deal much with self disputation anyway, but Shakespeare is making Juliet's reasoning serve to convince the audience as well as herself. Two courses were open to her on receipt of the terrible news. She could deny her husband or excuse him. At first she was not sure which to do, but after the brilliant passage of *oxymora*, in which she said the worst that she could say about him, she knew that she had to excuse him. It was right and also reasonable. Insofar as she is attempting to put the audience into a frame of mind consistent with her purpose, the figure is one of pathos, but insofar as she is offering herself a reason strong enough to vanquish all objections, Romeo is alive and Tybalt would have slain him, it resembles the figure *pareuresis*, though it is also a disjunctive *enthymeme*. The means of making the statement, however, is another sort of figure entirely, *chiasmus*, built around a crossing of the words *husband* and *slain*. How Shakespeare named his figures of argument we cannot know, or even that he had names for them, and the handbooks do not help us very much. Most of their examples are wooden compared to Shakespeare's practices, and that is what we should expect, for Shakespeare would have been encouraged in the school to form figures more subtle than the textbook examples, whether they actually came from Puttenham or Sherry or from some Latin work. But it really does not matter how he would have spoken about Juliet's rationalization in this speech; it seems indisputable he intended it to be a combination of figures and thus a proper part of rhetoric.

It is interesting to notice how quickly Juliet proceeds from the passage packed with *oxymora* to rational thought, leading to a correct conclusion, even though to excuse Romeo was the conclusion she wanted to reach and even though she mitigated it somewhat when she thought of banishment. Juliet rises through her use of figures to meet the occasion. To the Elizabethan proper use of rhetoric was a noble thing. Romeo was not so quick about it. He went to Friar Laurence after the slaying of Tybalt a man broken in spirit ready to "sack / The hateful mansion" (III.iii.107-108); that is, to commit suicide. The priest upbraided him, "Fie, fie, thou shamest thy shape, thy love, thy wit" (line 122), and then he offered him substantially the same rationalization Juliet was able to reach by herself: "Tybalt would kill thee, / But thou slewest Tybalt: there art thou happy" (lines 137-138). Romeo was to be convinced by an array of reasons, not all of them perhaps related to the clear thinking of the friar. A way was being offered him to consummate the marriage. It took some argument to convince him, but finally he admitted, "How well my comfort is revived by this!" (line 165). In fact Friar Laurence's argument lasted nearly fifty lines. When one compares the passages, it almost seems as if Shakespeare implied that in the terrible crises of life the woman shows the most strength (certainly she is the quickest to revive). And indeed from the banishment to the end of the play, excepting only one great scene with Juliet, some sixty lines at the beginning of Act III, scene v, before the entrance of Lady Capulet, Romeo's course is fairly steadily downwards towards his tragic end. Accident intervenes momentarily when the letter from Friar Laurence goes astray. Romeo buys poison from the apothecary. He hastens to Verona, meets Paris at the entrance to the Capulet monument and reluctantly slays him. He finds Juliet seemingly dead and slays himself before he has time to discover the truth. By this time his tragic death is inevitable, and we have reached the end of the play. After the death of the innocent Paris there was no possible chance of commuting Romeo's sentence. He was marked for death no matter what he found in the tomb.

Juliet presents a sharp contrast, in line with the character Shakespeare carefully delineated in the scene where she received the news of Tybalt's death (and of course elsewhere in the play). She takes the drug, though she is permitted to doubt Friar Laurence's motives for a moment. Terrified, but not blenching at the prospect, she goes to face the horrors of the charnel house, where she knows the body of her cousin was recently deposited. For Juliet it was at the best a desperate solution. Finally, when she awakes to find Romeo dead beside her, when she understands that all is lost, she slays herself for love. Juliet has suffered most in the play. She has had to face the grave peril of being forced into adultery and bigamy. She has lost her world, her parents, her lover, and finally she risks losing love itself, for she cannot be sure that the end of grand passion is a victory. Her trials have been greater than his, and accordingly it seems that her victory should be the greater. There is little need for rhetoric to help explain these ideas to the audience, for the end of the play has been reached. Truly it is time for plain speaking at last, but the devices do not altogether disappear. Shakespeare still allows Juliet a last example of *prosopopoeia*: "O churl,

drunk all, and left no friendly drop / To help me after"
(V.iii.163-164). But there is nothing more for the rhetoric
to accomplish. The characterization is over; the plot is
finished.

Sometimes it almost seems Shakespeare spent himself on
the statement of the problem and reserved little energy for
the solution (he gives a similar impression in *Julius Caesar*
and *Hamlet*, for he had not yet solved all the problems of
writing tragedy), but that opinion is a distortion. Figures are
naturally more essential at the beginning of a play where the
author wishes to indicate character and develop action. One
cannot exactly prove that contention by counting them, for
the way the figures are used, not their number, matters. Only
in context, by a qualitative examination, is one likely to
ascertain the part figures play in the structure of the drama.
Draper, for example, has noted that Juliet, by and large, has
fewer figures than Romeo,[19] but that observation is meaningless until we examine the actual occurrences themselves.
Then it will appear that with respect to the most important
figure in the play, *oxymoron*, Juliet is Romeo's superior. After
Juliet's performance with this figure, the device disappears
from the play, though there are some hints of it if not clear-
cut examples. That is as it should be. *Oxymoron* has func-
tioned as an important clue to theme and structure of the
play. Shakespeare used it particularly to define the characters
of first Romeo and then Juliet and to indicate some slight
though important differences between their respective roles.
He also used it to emphasize and often clarify the theme of
appearance and reality on which much of the play depends.

Oxymoron was the appropriate figure for *Romeo and Juliet*.
By wrenching together disparate elements to make a single
whole, it serves well to symbolize the collision of those planets
Venus and Mars. At the same time it reminds us that the
tragedy that ensues was not really a matter of astral accident
but only seems so. The tragedy arises primarily from char-

acter, but Romeo and Juliet were not tried and convicted for an excess of passion, or because Juliet defied her parents' wishes, or for any such reason. They have only the flaws of youth and love and life—theirs is the tragedy of life. Romeo has many faces if only the one name Montague. Juliet is even more complex. They are people doomed not because they give way to love, for their love is a grand passion, and that is excusable even in tired, cynical lovers (*Antony and Cleopatra*). Nor are they doomed because they are Veronese and live in a milieu hostile to love. In fact Verona and England (and the rest of the world) are the same in that respect. They are doomed because life is tragic for people of their sensibilities. Love should conquer all, but usually in the real world violence wins.

Both Romeo and Juliet are masterful manipulators of figures. It is the measure of their intellects and a mark of the transcendence of the intellectual portions of their souls above the others. It is also part of their humour, as well. For example, Juliet on the whole is sanguine; that is, she is choleric 'under the benign influence of the sun, a humour that approximated the sanguine."[20] But under the stress of certain emotion her intellect is sharpened, and perhaps she rises above her humour, too. Her virtuoso performance with *oxymora* really sets her character, especially with relation to Romeo. But if Juliet is Romeo's master, as I contend, then Shakespeare is still the master of them both. The play is a breathtaking experiment with figures of rhetoric (as well as with mixed genre), and so far as anyone can tell it worked marvelously well. Shakespeare was attempting to write a tragedy that arises out of character without seriously flawing the principals. Romeo and Juliet are brought to their ends mainly because life is a violent experience and great love a fragile thing within it. All this works even now for us, with our limited appreciation of the devices that must have made it such exciting theatre for the Elizabethans.

CHAPTER THREE

The Osier Cage

THE BALCONY SCENE in *Romeo and Juliet,* surely the greatest love scene in the history of the theatre, ends by coming full circle, to restate Romeo's proposition when he first saw Juliet leaning over the balcony, her cheek resting upon her hand: "O, that I were a glove upon that hand" (II.i.66). In his final speech, when the scene is finished, he repeats that note:

> Sleep dwell upon thine eyes, peace in thy breast!
> Would I were sleep and peace, so sweet to rest!
> Hence will I to my ghostly friar's cell,
> His help to crave and my dear hap to tell.
>
> (II.i.229-232)

The effect of Romeo's statement, charmingly sensual as it is, resembles that of the figure *prosopopoeia* (wherein an inanimate object or abstract thing is represented as having personal characteristics; that is, a kind of personification), one of Shakespeare's favorite rhetorical devices.[1] But in the very extravagance of the restatement it is also *hyperbolic.* As so often happens in Shakespeare, there is a complexity of figures in the couplet beginning "Sleep dwell upon thine eyes," after which the scene ends with Romeo's telling the audience in a matter-of-fact way where he is going.

We should not forget that Shakespeare had neither lights nor curtains. If he had, the last couplet, which breaks the tone of the speech, might have been unnecessary. There has been some argument over the placing of the balcony scene on stage, but whatever the correct interpretation, it had to take place at the back of the platform where the upper level could somehow be used. And, as the key scene in the entire play, it commands absolute attention. When it was over Juliet withdrew and Romeo departed for the confessor's cell. The action must then come forward on to the platform, and for the first time we are introduced to Friar Laurence.

Shakespeare's introduction is masterfully efficient and serves as direct contrast to the heightened tension of the great love scene. The text makes it clear that the audience was not immediately shown the friar's cell, probably the inner stage, and the entire following scene may be played quite effectively at the front of the platform. We find Friar Laurence approaching the audience, gathering herbs on the hillside. Some twenty lines later, after Shakespeare has allowed him time to get away from the Capulet orchard, Romeo encounters him, possibly after a quick exit and entrance. The contrast with the previous scene, so important to the delicate balance of the dramatic structure, is emphasized in several subtle ways. First and most obvious, the action has physically shifted on the stage. Then, the friar's character, because he is a holy man, a characteristic that could be quickly indicated by his costume, casts a different mood over the play. Coleridge thought of that when he commented on this introduction, "The reverend character of the Friar, like all Shakespeare's representations of the great professions, is very delightful and tranquilizing, yet it is no digression, but immediately necessary to the carrying on of the plot."[2] The last part of his statement seems to refer particularly to the gathering of herbs.

But there are further links between the scene at Juliet's balcony and the next, carefully planned so that the transition will not be too abrupt. When we first notice the friar "alone, with a basket" (a stage direction that does not appear in any of the quartos or the *Folio* but that is commonly added after Malone), he addresses the audience:

> The grey-eyed morn smiles on the frowning night,
> Chequ'ring the eastern clouds with streaks of light;
> And flecked darkness like a drunkard reels
> From forth day's path and Titan's fiery wheels.
> Now, ere the sun advance his burning eye,
> The day to cheer and night's dank dew to dry,
> I must up-fill this osier cage of ours
> With baleful weeds and precious juiced flowers.
> The earth that's nature's mother is her tomb:
> What is her burying grave, that is her womb.
>
> (II.iii.1-10)

(The speech continues for 12 more lines, mostly devoted to the chemistry of love potions.) Again the effect is that of *prosopopoeia* rather extravagantly done. The personifications of morn and night and darkness provide a direct link with Romeo's final lines in the previous scene, but there is of course an immense difference between the speech of Romeo and that of Friar Laurence. For one thing the friar is no poet; Shakespeare says so by placing in his mouth worn cliches and overly conceited phrases: *grey-eyed morn, Titan's fiery wheels, dank dew*, etc. Surely these are enough to prove the point. Nor is Friar Laurence a masterful rhetorician, despite the attractiveness of some of his devices. He is not meant to be either; that is not his role in the play. Instead, as Coleridge noticed, he is tranquilizing, one whose speech is not devoid of figures but a character who shows no sign of the magnificent touch of wit that Romeo or Juliet (or to a lesser degree Benvolio or Mercutio) could command at will.

It would seem that Friar Laurence's role in the play has been too long neglected. Excepting Coleridge, most critics are content to dismiss him with a phrase or two. Thus

Granville-Barker says, "As a man of affairs, poor Friar Laurence proved deplorable, but he had imagination"[3] (that last perhaps slightly ironic). H. C. Goddard thinks that, as Romeo's ghostly confessor, the friar is structurally contrasted with Juliet's nurse.[4] Both critics are perceptive and both are right, but remarks of this nature are too brief to explain such an important character in the play. Though his role is confined largely to three scenes, Friar Laurence is roughly as necessary to the development of the drama as Mercutio, and Shakespeare leaves to him the peroration. He is not so attractive as the volatile Mercutio, but in the list of personages that contribute to the action he should be placed ahead of Benvolio, the Capulets, certainly the Prince himself, and probably the nurse.

After the personifications, which are quite ordinary by comparison with Romeo's, Friar Laurence's speech turns to an arresting paradox, the idea that the earth is the mother of generation as well as its tomb. That idea was thoroughly familiar to writers in the Renaissance (see Spenser's *Faerie Queene*, III.vi.33f: "After that they again returned beene, / They in that Gardin planted be againe; / And grow afresh . . ."). By comparison with Spenser Friar Laurence's treatment of the idea is somewhat muddled, and it is certainly expressed in a turgid couplet. But the statement of the paradox does serve to indicate the meditative nature of the friar, and accordingly perhaps helps to account for his deplorable management of the affairs of the lovers. Despite the fact that some critics think otherwise, Friar Laurence is not very worldly-wise,[5] except perhaps about the sexual conduct of the youth of Verona. Indeed, only the young, Romeo and Juliet and Paris, go to his cell for confession; there is no indication in the play that he has any professional contact whatsoever with older heads. Whether he is a trifle childish in his simplicity or whether Shakespeare was using him to

scoff gently at *contemptus mundi* is hard to say, but in any
case he is certainly not the person to find a solution for these
lovers threatened by the cruel society of Verona.

But Friar Laurence is not altogether simple minded, even
though at times it seems he wishes us to think so. His mind
in fact turns often to complexities, though they seldom have
very much relation to the reality of the outer world. His
conceited phraseology is by no means simple: *chequ'ring the
eastern clouds, flecked darkness, dank dew, osier cage. Osier
cage,* indeed! Why does he not come out and say willow
basket? Does his very language perhaps indicate a devious
turn of mind, dramatically necessary to the person who gave
Juliet the sleeping potion that directly brought about the
dreadful conclusion? By his speech we shall know him, and
even this holy friar is not quite what he seems, Shakespeare
reminds us, conjuring again with the theme of appearance
and reality that runs delicately through the play.

There are other things in Friar Laurence's first speech, as
Coleridge saw, that point forward to the action of the play.
At the very simplest level the gathering of herbs qualifies him
for preparing the sleeping draught that causes a resemblance
to death. There is a careful attention paid to probability and
verisimilitude. But Friar Laurence says more than he himself
could possibly have understood:

> Two such opposed kings encamp them still
> In man as well as herbs, grace and rude will;
> And where the worser is predominant,
> Full soon the canker death eats up the plant.
>   (II.ii.27-30)

Here the language seems somewhat platitudinous, and I
think it is likely to prove misleading. Such talk adds ammuni-
tion to the guns of those that believe Romeo and Juliet come
to their tragic end because of an excess of passion in their

characters. That is really what Friar Laurence would seem to be implying, but the passage occurs long before we have any direct hint of what is going to happen, while it is still fair for Shakespeare to suggest any possibility. Besides, Friar Laurence is not an entirely credible witness. In this highly psychological passage Shakespeare seems to be suggesting that tragedy could arise from an excess of passion, perhaps even that Friar Laurence would be the sort of man to think so. But in fact their passion does not directly bring about the tragedy that befalls Romeo and Juliet, except in the sense that if it had not existed nothing at all would have happened.

That their love is a grand passion has already been made clear in the balcony scene. It transcends ordinary concerns, and though highly sensual and erotic it is not sinful. In *Romeo and Juliet* "the divinity of Love is the thing; this it is that is to be represented, an ideal passion. Even here there is, besides this passion, the world without . . ."[6] which the friar scarcely understands. He is expert only at body chemistry and herbs. That Shakespeare meant us to take his words at face value, to imply that the ending arose from an excess of passion, as it might for ordinary mortals, seems unthinkable when we consider the friar's role in the play. There is another sense, though, in which the friar's words suggest the dual themes of the play, those of love and war, and hint at the outcome. Violence leads to death. In this sense Shakespeare permits the friar to say more to the audience than he himself could understand. A little change, almost suggested by the language itself, would make it even plainer. Suppose Shakespeare had written "two such opposed *camps*" instead of "two such opposed *kings* encamp them still?" A hint of the feud between the Montagues and the Capulets, with all of the dreadful horror that entails, lies just beneath the surface of the language.

All this takes place just before Romeo greets Friar Laurence.

After Romeo speaks, the mood alters. The personifications do not disappear ("And where care lodges, sleep will never lie," II.ii.36), but the friar's attention is directed to Romeo's entrance on the stage. He speculates about the cause of the visit: "then here I hit it right, / Our Romeo hath not been in bed to-night." On the whole the flavor of the speech is aphoristic; it is not really very worldly despite the conclusion Friar Laurence jumps to, encouraged perhaps by the ambiguity of Romeo's answer, that Romeo has finally succeeded with Rosaline. "God pardon sin," he says, where a more tough minded priest might have said, "For shame! Thou hast fallen into sin!" We cannot quite take him seriously as a confessor; he is instead the confidant of young lovers. He is puzzled when Romeo answers his speculation about Rosaline with, "No, I have forgot that name." The exchange is filled with charm and subtle dramatic excitement, partly because the audience is already beginning to identify with Romeo and partly because it is privy to the situation and can enjoy the friar's discomfiture. But there is more involved than just our knowledge that Juliet has utterly replaced Rosaline in Romeo's affections. Romeo's language troubles the friar, who is no match for him at the game of wit, forcing him to complain: "Be plain, good son, and homely in thy drift: / Riddling confession finds but riddling shrift."

This complaint, lightly tendered as it is, is important in distinguishing the friar's role in the play, for despite an arresting remark now and then he is quite incapable of engaging in word games with Romeo. In that respect he is not the counterpart of the nurse, who fares better, though perhaps unwittingly, in her exchanges with Juliet. Friar Laurence is a good chemist, an encourager of young love, a man of peace who loaths violence, a man courageous enough to oppose the law, but one not especially well fitted for intellectual pursuits. He is certainly not helpless rhetorically,

Shakespeare would hardly show a member of the clergy in that light, but wit, that representative of reason at which Romeo and Juliet both excel, is beyond his powers. He is better at the role he prefers to assume, that of a plain simple man, than he is at disputation or at settling feuds or marriages. A naïveté in his nature makes him think of preparing a death-like sleeping potion for Juliet rather than seeking a direct means of saving her from a bigamous marriage. Juliet was never in a position to confess the secret marriage to Romeo to her father, whose ire shielded him from the truth, but Friar Laurence might have entreated for her. Such a meeting, however, was beyond his power. Instead he acted illegally, and, what is worse, bungled.

Also he fails to understand Romeo. He is accustomed to hearing about trifling affairs of the heart, which he seems to recognize as sexually motivated. A man must learn something at the confessional. But when he is faced with great passion, he is unable to recognize it. When Romeo tries to explain, he chides him:

> Holy Saint Francis! What a change is here!
> Is Rosaline, that thou didst love so dear,
> So soon forsaken? Young men's love then lies
> Not truly in their hearts, but in their eyes.
> (II.ii.65-68)

He scoffs at the doctrine of love at first sight, which Shakespeare, perhaps borrowing it from Marlowe's *Hero and Leander* (after all he made his own attempt at that genre, the erotic epyllion, in *Venus and Adonis*), used as a means to great passion. In his gentle way the friar almost seems to be accusing Romeo of lust of the eye. It is hard to blame him for being deceived, for on the surface Romeo is the most fickle of lovers. Still, we cannot help thinking the friar, of all people, should have known better. Romeo is not really light;

he is serious and intellectual, sensitive and capable of the deepest affection, and his confessor at least might have recognized the nature of the change that had come over him. Instead he chides Romeo with empty aphorisms: "Women may fall when there's no strength in men" (II.ii.80). When Romeo complains that this love for Juliet is different because it is requited, something a confessor can certainly understand, Friar Laurence turns opportunist and thinks how he can use the situation to mend the feud in Verona. It is a naïve idea, and it does not take into account what has really happened to Romeo. The friar promises help but ends with another aphorism, cautioning Romeo to be careful: "Wisely and slow: they stumble that run fast" (II.ii.94).

When next we see Friar Laurence in the short scene before the wedding (scene 5 in Act II), he repeats this aphorism: "Therefore love moderately: long love doth so" (II.v.14). Thus the scenes are connected and Shakespeare's deliberate characterization of the friar (whom he altered considerably from the source) reemphasized. Unable to understand the demands or even the nature of grand passion, the friar falls back again on clichés, a habit of speech that may endear him to the audience but says nothing for him as a rational man desirous of mending the world. Still, we should not lose patience with the friar too quickly; to Shakespeare gnomic wisdom was often true wisdom, and Friar Laurence's advice is sound for all except the most exceptional of lovers. Perhaps that interesting and unusual compound *long love* was calculated to make that point. The speech, short as it is, ends with yet another aphorism: "Too swift arrives as tardy as too slow" (line 15). Whatever else Shakespeare is doing, he is stacking the cards to point forward to a tragic ending of the play that the friar cannot suspect. Not knowing grand passion, Friar Laurence does not understand that it is always a risky thing (in literature nearly always fatal). That it may contain its own special victory is entirely beyond his experience; he will only be in a position to speculate about that at the end of the play and then only if he is kept on stage.

Actually Friar Laurence is given only a few lines in the short pre-nuptial scene that ends the second act. The real matter of the scene belongs to Juliet, when she makes her sole comment on the rhetoric of her lover. Romeo, swept away with enthusiasm by the proximity of consummation of his love, addresses her:

> Ah, Juliet, if the measure of thy joy
> Be heaped like mine, and that thy skill be more
> To blazon it, then sweeten with thy breath
> This neighbor air, and let rich music's tongue
> Unfold the imagined happiness that both
> Receive in either by this dear encounter.
> (II.v.24-29)

This is an altogether remarkable invitation, constructed with a total lack of end stopped lines, as if to say Romeo is breathless at his prospects. He addresses her respectfully and charmingly if somewhat extravagantly, inviting her to break into song, as they had in their duet at the ball, but Juliet surprises him:

> Conceit, more rich in matter than in words,
> Brags of his substance, not of ornament.
> They are but beggars that can count their worth;
> But my true love is grown to such excess,
> I cannot sum up sum of half my wealth.
> (II.v.30-34)

The time has come, Juliet reminds him, for love's seriousness. Grand passion is never frivolous. And here again there is mention of excess, but this time Juliet has turned the idea. She is speaking of an excess of true love, which cannot be

tragic fault. For Juliet love is a virtue, and there can never
be too much virtue. But even more interesting are the first
two lines of her reply. I read a full stop after *ornament*,
following several editors, but nearly all employ at least a colon
at that place. In any case there is a distinct break in the
subject matter of the speech, after which Juliet permits her
thoughts to run to the nature of her love for Romeo. Craik,
in *The English of Shakespeare*,[7] understands *conceit* "to denote her all absorbing affection for Romeo." He equates
Juliet's choice of terms with the scriptural expression "wise
in his own conceit," which, he says, means only wise in his
own thought. He cites Shakespeare's use of the word *conceit*
in *The Merchant of Venice* and *Love's Labour's Lost* and
arrives at the conclusion—in my opinion quite erroneous—
that Juliet is sweetly if a little indirectly agreeing with Romeo,
or perhaps praising him for putting the subject of their love
that way. The definition on which the commentator is
depending is that of *conceit* as sentiment as distinguished
from imagery, a definition cited in the *OED*. But, it seems
to me, that Juliet means by *conceit* a fanciful, witty notion, or
expression (a definition reported as early as 1581). That
definition is closely related to the modern one of *conceit* as
excessive metaphor, and about that Juliet is warning Romeo.
Romeo's invitation to Juliet to make sweet music with him,
to put it vulgarly, is an example of cultivated obscurity,
conceptismo, an aspect of *Marinism, precositié, Schwulst*,
however Shakespeare may have called it. As such it is not
bad; it is sometimes to be admired but not in its present
context. No amount of language will serve to make their love
exceptional, Juliet is reminding him; to begin with, it must
be that. Almost from its inception, Juliet recognized the
extraordinary nature of their relationship, and her business
has been to instruct Romeo in it. In the balcony scene she
asked him not to swear his fidelity, the usual way of pledging

troth. Now she reminds him that precious language has nothing to do with their love, though there is no sign that she has any innate prejudice against verbal ornament. In fact she is very good at it herself. But in this moment of truth there is no need for Romeo to tell her to sweeten the air with her breath in a love song. He is still playing at the game of courtship; Juliet is beyond it. For her their love is already a divine thing. Thus she chides him gently for the excesses of his language. But it is not rhetoric to which she is objecting, but rather over subtlety at the wrong moment. Perhaps in her phrase there is even a gentle apology for the whole rhetorical method of the play.

After the hasty pre-nuptial scene Friar Laurence does not appear again on stage until Romeo comes to his cell after the slaying of Tybalt to discover the Prince's judgment. Then the friar plays his greatest scene in the play, which begins in a leisurely fashion. The friar, fully aware of the seriousness of banishment, much more serious to people of the Renaissance than it seems to us, breaks the news slowly, beginning with a somewhat aphoristic, portentous statement. "Thou art wedded to calamity," he says (III.iii.3). Even so, he is surprised by Romeo's reaction, which must seem stronger than the circumstances warrant. As yet the friar has no appreciation of the immediacy of an unconsummated grand passion. "Here from Verona art thou banished," he explains. "Be patient for the world is broad and wide" (lines 15-16). The aphorism, the friar is still dealing in his usual stock in trade, is a useless sop to Romeo, for to him "there is no world without Verona's wall . . . Heaven is here / Where Juliet lives" (lines 16, 29, 30). And we, the audience, have come to accept Romeo's appraisal of the situation, though the friar's attitude is that of common sense. Why should Romeo not go to Mantua and take Juliet with him? But Shakespeare had made Juliet fourteen, old enough for a secret marriage but perhaps too young for an elopement. It does not really matter, for Shakespeare was bound in factual matters by his source. He made Romeo's reaction to banishment appear reasonable to the audience (an easier job with an Elizabethan audience than with a modern one) by leading them to understand that Romeo and Juliet were bound by grand passion; the friar never quite understood that.

He tries again to comfort Romeo by offering him, aphoristically, "adversity's sweet milk, philosophy," but Romeo will have none of it. "Hang up philosophy," he answers; we should say "Hang philosophy." "Hang up philosophy unless philosophy can make a Juliet" (lines 57-58, q.v.). At this point Friar Laurence abandons aphorism; he has learned that Romeo is not to be pacified with sayings. In a sense he can no longer deal with an unruly adolescent but must face a man, and he must do so in the ways of men. After an interlude with the nurse, who enters at this point, giving the friar a chance to marshal his arguments, he tries rhetoric. "Let me dispute with thee of thy estate," he says to Romeo, just before the knock on the door, and when he returns to the subject after the interruption he has had a chance to gather his thoughts. As an exponent of disputation, or rhetoric, he reaches his highest point in the play. His is a noble effort and perhaps partially successful, even in the face of Romeo's desperation.

Romeo threatens to slay himself, and the friar begins his argument:

> Art thou a man? Thy form crys out thou art.
> Thy tears are womanish; thy wild acts denote
> The unreasonable fury of a beast.
> Unseemly woman in a seeming man!
> And ill-beseeming beast in seeming both!

I take this figure to be a rough kind of *enthymeme*, an attempt at logical reasoning, though it does not much resemble the examples furnished by rhetoricians when they consider *aetio-logia*, for it "combines antithesis with inference and works out two opposing arguments in a small space."[8] It seems a little akin to Portia's, "God made him, and therefore let him pass for a man" (*Merchant of Venice*, I.ii.60). The friar is saying, your tears are womanish, your acts bestial, get hold of yourself and behave like a rational being; moreover, he is implying, if Romeo does not there cannot be any solution to the problem. Again the theme is appearance and reality.

The rest of the speech is a closely reasoned argument constructed around the idea "Tybalt would kill thee, / But thou slewest Tybalt" (lines 137-138), the self defense argument, and it is a brilliant example both of argumentation and of the use of figures. Because of it Friar Laurence rises in our estimation, and none too soon in the play. For a man so easily contented with aphorisms to rise to such a height of rhetoric must have required a supreme effort, and we must not fail to appreciate it. Of course, Romeo is proving exceptionally difficult. This time he is really suffering from an excess of passion, and it is not love. Rather it is a mixture of remorse, frustration, and sorrow brought about because he has equated the death of Tybalt with the death of love. Not only is he suffering because the marriage remains unconsummated, but he is afraid Juliet may denounce him for the deed he unwittingly committed. And *unwittingly* is the right adverb. For an instant Romeo stepped from the world of love and wit, from his world of reason, into the violent, adult world of Verona, and chaos descended upon him. To forget love but a moment is to reap the whirlwind. Now the friar must work a rhetorical miracle to restore some semblance of reason to his distracted brain.

At about this point (in the action of the play) Juliet, too, has begun to change, to rise above her lover in strength of character. Of course their circumstances are quite different, but both are sorely beset by the outer world and in real danger. Unlike Romeo, Juliet must face her tribulations alone. Romeo needs a long scolding speech by the friar, and then he is only partly convinced. We are concerned here with that speech, which is a masterful production in the art of persuasion. Its figures, primarily devices of repetition, are used to heighten and enforce the argument (and the emotion that accompanies it), and each of the major ones is magnified far out of proportion to usual textbook examples. First, there is *anastrophe* (that is, return; the use at the beginning of a clause of the phrase that ended the preceeding one: e.g. "He has a lust for *blood. Blood* shall fill his cup"), or perhaps Shakespeare thought of it as *epanastrophe,* which is closely related. "Why railest thou on thy *birth, the heaven and earth?* / Since *birth and heaven and earth,* all three do meet / In thee at once. . . ." (III.iii.119-121) (Italics mine.) Several other figures are also suggested by this passage. In the first line *asyndeton* (absence of conjunction), for example, or perhaps one would think of it as *polysyndeton* (the repetition of conjunction) in the second line. And there is a distinct reminder of *hysteron proteron* (reversal of chronological order) in the unclimactic arrangement of *birth, heaven,* and *earth* (though probably rhetoricians would not care for this as an example). Clearly the passage is very complex rhetorically.

There follows shortly afterwards *epistrophe* (a figure in which sentences or clauses end with the same word or some-times phrase):

> Fie, fie, thou shamest *thy shape, thy love, thy wit:*
> Which, like a usurer, abound'st in all,
> And usest none in that true use indeed
> Which should bedeck *thy shape, thy love, thy wit.*
> (III.iii.122-125)

(Italics mine.) As in the example of *anastrophe* immediately preceding, there are three elements involved; that is, three substantives instead of the usual one, demonstrating Shakespeare's (and in this moment of great stress Friar Laurence's) virtuosity. But this time in contrast to the former figure the order of the substantives is climactic. That is as it should be, for the friar is telling Romeo that his conduct brings shame on the whole man, the body (shape), the will or affections (love), and the reason (wit).

Epistrophe is closely followed by *paranomasia* (that is, play on words, the word in this case *shape*), though perhaps Shakespeare would have considered it *antanaclasis* (a figure in which the repeating word shifts its meaning). The lines that follow read, "Thy noble *shape* is but a form of wax, / Digressing from the valour of a man" (italics mine). Not only is the word *shape* changed from its previous meaning *body* to include the whole man (equivalent perhaps to *soul*, or *body* and *soul*), but there is an additional play on the word *wax*, which is deliberately ambiguous to indicate Romeo's weakness under adversity and also to remind us of the Platonic doctrine of the tripartite soul, on which the previous figure partly depends. The analogy of the soul to a block of wax was thoroughly familiar to Renaissance writers. A rather neat balance is maintained as the speech continues. Friar Laurence devotes two lines to Romeo's injury to shape, two to the injury he is doing to love, and four (quite proper in terms of emphasis) to the injury to wit (that is, reason, the highest part of man).

A few lines later the argument is continued with a further example of *epistrophe*, one almost as impressive as the great terminal repetition in Antony's funeral oration, "And Brutus is an honorable man."

> Thy Juliet is alive,
> For whose dear sake thou wast but lately dead:
> *There art thou happy.* Tybalt would kill thee,
> But thou slewest Tybalt: *there art thou happy.*

The law, that threatened death, becomes thy friend,
And turns it to exile: *there art thou happy.*

(III.iii.135-140)

(Italics mine.) The terminal repetition occurs three times, in balance with the rest of the speech. It is very neat and reaches an irrefutable conclusion. At least that is the way I read the passage and the way I am convinced Romeo understood it. We should probably have said, "There—thou canst not be aught but happy" or "There, that must make you happy." It would be a mistake to read the repetition as a rhetorical question (the editors do not use that punctuation) as I suspect is often done, for it is not part of the argument but the conclusion to which the friar has been driving Romeo. The speech is one of *pathos*, where one endeavours to place the listener into a frame of mind favorable to his own purpose,[9] and the passage above also contains another sort of figure, *anamnesis* (recital of past events, usually woes or injuries). Much the same thing may be seen in *Richard III*: "I had an Edward, till a Richard killed him; / I had a Harry, till a Richard killed him," etc. (IV.iv.36-37), except there instead of a complex of *anamnesis* and *epistrophe* the combination is with *symploce* (a name usually used to denote a combination of the repetitions of *anaphora* with those of *epistrophe*).

Afterwards the tone of the passage changes. The conclusion having been drawn, it may be reinforced by a sort of *philophronesis* (mitigating speech), and that is exactly what happens. Line 141 reads, "A pack of blessings lights upon thy back." The friar has done all he could for Romeo. He has mustered all his wit (his reason) and his rhetorical training, much more than we should have dreamed him capable of, to talk Romeo out of his threatened self-destruction, a threat brought about by black melancholy, that vile humour, that followed Romeo's one misstep into the adult world of violence. The rest of the speech turns to practical considerations; Romeo will spend that night with Juliet, consummate the marriage, and flee to Mantua with the dawn. The nurse must return quickly to her mistress to bid her prepare for the bridegroom.

The entire speech has been magnificent. Not only has the friar shown himself capable of a superb effort, but he has succeeded in persuading Romeo to abandon his black despair, though ironically Shakespeare leaves the matter a little ambiguous. Perhaps it is the plan for the ensuing night that really turns the trick. The play indeed is a love story. Romeo himself does not comment on Friar Laurence's rhetoric, though there is no reason to believe he did not understand it perfectly. The speech was emotionally heightened and entirely serious, and it was certainly devoted to a noble purpose, but Shakespeare is often impatient with people who step out of character. He does not quite let the friar off unscathed. Perhaps he cannot afford to, for the friar's bungling is still going to be important in the development of the tragedy. After he has finished, the nurse lets some of the wind out of his sails: "O, what learning is!" she exclaims.

Attention here has been directed to figures of words rather than sense, for those are what Shakespeare placed in prominent position in the friar's speech, but I have already pointed out that the speech is a rhetorical complex. The argument itself was important whether or not it finally convinced Romeo. We should not assume that Shakespeare was essentially a figurist rhetorician, rather than a traditionalist or a Ramist. In fact he used whatever methods he required, and anyhow all three schools overlap in their approach to the same ends. One might go a little further. Wilson recommended that at the end of a speech the speaker should "stirre the hearers to bee sorie, *to bee glad,* or to bee offended"[10] (italics mine), and that is the advice Friar Laurence seems to have followed when he drew his conclusion, "There art thou happy." There are other figures involved in the complex, too. For example, the speech begins with a question, "Why railest thou on thy birth . . . ?" There are signs here of *epiplexis* or *percontatio* (asking a question not to find out something but to chide), even stronger when the friar asks, "Art thou a man?"[11]

We have been examining Friar Laurence's great speech in the play, and I have pointed out Shakespeare manages it in highly rhetorical terms. By clever manipulation of figures he lifts the friar out of his normal speech patterns, so highly dependent on aphorisms, and out of his usual character.[12] We next meet the friar at the beginning of the fourth act where he is in conference first with Paris, then with Paris and Juliet together, and finally with Juliet alone. In this scene he counsels Juliet, whom he now addresses as his "pensive daughter," to drink the distilling liquor which brings about a drowsy humour counterfeiting death. At the best this is a desperate plan, and though it has a certain subtlety it is proposed in language that is essentially plain and unornamented, despite a few metaphors in the lines. There is no need to persuade Juliet, whose alternatives have been evaporating.

The scene in fact lacks emotional intensity. It stands in contrast with the friar's last scene in which he revived hope in Romeo and sent him on his way to Juliet's bedchamber. A good deal has happened since then. The Capulets have insisted on an overhasty marriage to the County Paris. The friar previously thought he could cope with the Prince's displeasure. He hoped to settle the feud and defeat the outer world of violence that was Verona. But then he had to face parental management of a marriage; he had to interfere where he had no business. It was almost more than he could bear and certainly more than he could have foreseen, and for a moment he was tempted to let the other world win and permit matters to take their course. "I hear thou must, and nothing may prorogue it, / On Thursday next be married to this County" (IV.i.48-49), he tells Juliet. This is speech of a man whose hopes have been shattered; it is language of resignation. Of course something must prorogue the marriage of Juliet to Paris, or Juliet will be plunged into mortal sin. If the friar did not understand that, he would be a worldly confessor indeed. But for a moment he cannot struggle harder. Then, he conceived the desperate plan to have Juliet feign death. The plan was, it seems to me, entirely in accord with his psychology; Friar Laurence throughout the play is a man who has trouble distinguishing appearance from reality.

The mood of such a scene seems to call naturally for a language largely devoid of ornament, for there is resignation and desperation here in place of heightened emotion. Thus the friar's speech seems to fit the dramatic occasion well. Throughout the scene Juliet, too, remains the pensive daughter, sad and thoughtful, but being Juliet she is not entirely bereft of her intellect (that is, her wit) as was her confessor. When she comes on stage to meet Paris, he addresses her as his wife, and she answers, "That may be, sir, when I may be a wife." It is a sad paradox, for Juliet certainly never intended to become Paris's wife under any circumstances. To her death was a preferred alternative. But she was not so sad she could not engage in a little private wordplay, which the friar would understand, at the expense of Paris. If there is to be even the remote possibility of a chance for Juliet, she must preserve her intellect. "That may be must be," Paris answers, and she restates the aphorism. "What must be shall be," surely adds an ironic inflection. Moreover, there is a sort of rhetorical irony, too, in her turning at this remark to an aphorism, because that is really Friar Laurence's method of solving, or perhaps escaping, problems. It is as if she has reminded him he is not devoid of responsibility in the dreadful situation. But Shakespeare does not permit that note to be taken up quite seriously; instead he gives the friar an ambiguous line, possibly the one witty line he speaks in the scene: "That's a certain text" (IV.i.22), he answers. The way the director and actor interpret that line for the audience must make a real difference in the way the friar's role is understood.

Juliet continues to bait Paris, who would apparently like to comfort her(though it must be the death of Tybalt he has in mind) and offer some pledge of his love. We are almost sorry for him, and surely we are supposed to share his discomfort, for he does not know enough to understand what is at stake. But of course even if he did, he would be no match for Juliet. The dialogue turns to the subject of her tear-stained face, and she twists it all to meanings clear enough to the friar and the audience but hidden from Paris. And she is literally a pensive daughter, for the scene is intellectual rather than emotional. Finally Juliet tires of it and asks the friar if she should return later. Naturally Paris takes the cue and departs, and then the dire plan is hatched.

While the scene is sad and depressing, and the friar is at first tempted like the nurse to countenance sin, the situation is not absolutely hopeless. Shakespeare again reminds us that fate is playing a heavy hand in these affairs, but he is not ready to permit his lovers to resign themselves. That I think is clear from the language, which is intellectual. Juliet is still capable of deliberation, and even the friar is not absolutely beaten. At least he makes that one sensible remark, "That's a certain text," showing that he understands Juliet's conversation with Paris. It is a hopeful sign, but the odds in the play have measurably changed. No longer do Romeo and Juliet, and love, have very much chance against the world.

Friar Laurence makes another brief appearance at Juliet's feigned deathbed and delivers a short speech (19 lines) in which he once more shows signs of the power he exhibited when he persuaded Romeo that all was not lost. The speech begins with a simple *epanalepsis* (repetition at the end of a clause of the word or phrase with which it begins): "Confusion's cure lives not / In these confusions" (IV.v.65-66), a figure also showing some of the attributes of *prosopopoeia* so typical of the friar. It proceeds to *antanaclasis* (wherein the repeated word shifts its meaning), an extended play on the meaning of the word *heaven*, which is repeated five times in three sentences (that is, nine verses). The friar then ends with another personification, "Yet nature's tears are reason's merriment," which is also aphoristic, and small consolation to the bereft parents.

The style in this short passage is curiously mixed, I think deliberately. The friar begins on a rhetorical note suited to the heightened emotion of the situation, ostensibly a death scene, and then moves to an extended play on words (the figure *antanaclasis*), hardly notable in its content and scarcely suited to the supposedly serious business. One cannot claim *antanaclasis* is best suited to banter; it is after all a figure of thought, but there are not here enough variations on the meaning of *heaven* to make it a brilliant figure. Heaven and the Capulets, he says, had part in the making of Juliet, who has now gone to heaven, and the Capulets have only themselves to blame (in a sense this is true), for their heaven (that is, their goal) was for her to make a suitable marriage. In the very construction of the figure along these lines the friar has reverted to his old aphoristic style. The whole speech, we must not forget, is a sort of lie, for the friar knows perfectly well that Juliet is not dead at all but only sleeping. He seizes the opportunity to chide the parents; the figure involved is *onedismus*, employed as Peacham recommended to upbraid an "adversary of ingratitude and impietie."[13] Indeed in Shakespeare's ethic the Capulets are guilty of several serious impieties, but the one referred to here is the arranged marriage. "The most you sought was her promotion, / For 'twas your heaven she should be advanced" (lines 71-72), he reminds them. The whole speech has a false ring to it and rightfully so, for it arises from a false situation. The friar has done a dreadful thing to the parents of Juliet, but his devious scheme was the only way the simple man could conceive to solve the problems of the lovers and ameliorate the violence of Verona. Had he been more capable of rational argument or had he had the courage to employ reason with the Capulets with the vehemence he used to persuade Romeo that all was not lost, the outcome might have been different. But that was not the friar's character, and I think the figures employed here emphasize his shortcomings. We know him to be well intended, but everyone, Shakespeare seems to be reminding us, knows the trouble well intended bunglers can cause. If we listen to this speech with attention to its figures, it must be with a rising sense of horror.

In the last two scenes of the play Friar Laurence is given some brief appearances on stage to explain events. First we see him with Friar John where the delay concerning the letter to Romeo is explained. Here accident has intervened, but it has clearly played a minor part. Had Romeo been less impatient the quarantine would hardly have mattered; at any rate it would not have proved fatal. Then, the friar holds a short conversation with Balthasar before entering the tomb to find Romeo already dead. "Romeo! O, pale! Who else? What, Paris, too? / And steeped in blood? Ah, what an unkind hour / Is guilty of this lamentable chance!" (V.iii.144-146) All the way to the monument fear has clutched at Friar Laurence's breast, and now the well meaning man must face the consequences of his bungling misjudgment. Romeo is dead, and all is irrevocably lost. And like the man he is Friar Laurence hastens to shed the burden of blame that attaches to him. Fortune, he says, has brought about the tragedy, but we know better. He repeats that idea, as if to convince himself, a little ambiguously in the next speech after Juliet has awakened: "A greater power than we can contradict / Hath thwarted our intents" (lines 153-154). (Surely he is not blaming God.) Then fear conquers him, and he flees the tomb leaving Juliet alone with the corpses. It is his moment of weakness; he is playing the role of a man but hardly that of a real ghostly confessor. The friar who throughout the play has shown shortcomings in the reasonable part of his soul now has his courage flag. He is an old man, and he is only an agent in the play. We should pity him, as the Veronese do, rather than censure him, as do certain of his critics. But in all fairness to them perhaps we should admit that if attention were not squarely focused on Juliet in her death scene, the friar might not come off so well.

It is hard to ascertain whether Friar Laurence understands his own part in the tragedy or realizes at all the extent to which he has been responsible. Shakespeare allows him only one more speech, a peroration in which he sums up what has taken place for the other persons on the scene, the two sets of parents and the Prince. For the play to reach its ending they must understand. That speech is exceedingly plain and matter of fact. There is a slight suggestion that accident was responsible, for it is always hard for the living to blame themselves after tragedy. There is some confession of the friar's cowardice, and then the all too human admission:

> And, if aught in this
> Miscarried by my fault, let my old life
> Be sacrificed some hour before his time
> Unto the rigor of severest law.
>
> (V.iii.265-268)

The lines serve partially to redeem the friar. They are both a disclaimer of responsibility and an acceptance of it, and they end on a courageous note. The Prince, recognizing human fraility, has only one remark for him before dismissing him from the play: "We still have known thee for a holy man." The Prince recognizes the friar's good intentions, but he cannot bring himself to utter a more consoling forgiveness. He is a ruler, after all, not a priest. But he will not blame the friar. He should have been wiser, but he was not. So we leave him undisposed of—perhaps to spend the rest of his life in penance for his part in the tragedy.

In a dramatic sense, however, Romeo and Juliet, not the friar, are responsible for the tragedy. They are the young lovers, intelligent far beyond the average and most unwise. They are not seriously flawed, in an Aristotelian sense, but, among other things, they have been too ready to listen to unwise counsel and have been caught up in the sweep of great emotions they could not control. Shakespeare could have left it at that, but he chose to go a short step further. There is in the monument to be erected to them in purest gold the hint that great passion, even though it ends in death, has its own glories. Love conquers even death. But the friar has no part in this nor any understanding of it. He has been woven into the texture of the play with great care to make events take place. His speech is the clue to his personality and often explains what the events must be and why they happen as they do. On the surface his role is an extremely minor one, but actually it is tremendously important. Shakespeare was not content to make him just an agent, the most important in the play, but instead through his words (and at the end through his action in abandoning Juliet) Shakespeare gave him a character. All this he built into the play carefully a small bit at a time. We saw the friar first with his willow basket collecting herbs, and perhaps that image of him with the "osier cage" is a direct clue to his part in the drama. He is woven into the play much as a basket is woven of willow strands. The basket is used to collect healing herbs or poisons.

So might Friar Laurence, depending on what he is, solve the problems of the lovers or cast them on the way to death. Shakespeare made him a little affected when he permitted him to speak for the first time, and perhaps that was to alert the audience to mark that character. Whether that was Shakespeare's intention or not, we cannot know for certain, but the play *Romeo and Juliet* without Friar Laurence would be very different.

CHAPTER FOUR

Mercutio's Apostrophe To Queen Mab

ONE OF THE MOST puzzling and difficult speeches to interpret in *Romeo and Juliet* is Mercutio's lengthy address to Queen Mab beginning at I.iv.53. For some forty-one lines Mercutio apostrophizes, until Romeo interrupts him with "Peace, peace, Mercutio, peace! / Thou talk'st of nothing." It is surprising how many critics have taken Romeo's ironic animadversion at face value, apparently concluding that Mercutio did indeed talk of nothing, at least nothing germane to the drama Shakespeare had been so carefully constructing. That is to say, they explain the speech as a digression in what is otherwise a tightly plotted and very closely dialogued play. The Queen Mab speech Granville-Barker concludes, "is as much and as little to be dramatically justified as a song in an opera is."[1] But perhaps he is carried away by the lyric quality of the play. He continues, in a footnote, to say that the scene as it is usually staged "needs attention. It is generally quite misunderstood and misinterpreted."[2]

Again, Schücking, as perceptive a critic as one is likely to find, calls our attention to a "clash of character and language in the case of Mercutio's speech about Queen Mab,"[3] and adds, later, that "no one will be surprised at the interruption of the dramatic unity who has paid attention to the frequent occurrence of similar transgressions of dramatic laws."[4] He continues to argue that the presumed digression is of the same order as Hamlet's references to the children's companies. It is the old argument, dressed rather more cautiously than usual, that Shakespeare neglected the unities. But Schücking is not talking about an important aspect of unity, such as time or place, which we all know Shakespeare handled in his own daring ways. He is drawing a parallel between a casual reference (a shot against the author's competitors) in *Hamlet* and a beautiful, poetic apostrophe in *Romeo and Juliet*. The very ineptness of the comparison should place us on guard.

If we examine these two statements more closely, it is evident that in at least one respect both Granville-Barker and Schücking are misleading. Moreover, they are not in agreement. Schücking says that no one will be upset by the violation he perceives to dramatic unity. He refers of course to the audience. On the other hand, Granville-Barker implies, by saying the scene needs attention, that people in the audience will be upset. Both critics are extending their arguments too far to score a point, and, it seems to me, it is quite likely that so far as the audience is concerned they may both be wrong. I should think that the Elizabethan audience found little violation of dramatic unity in the speech. Not that they would have minded if they had, for they were accustomed to all sorts of interruptions. But there is no reason to believe this speech was one of them, except Romeo's statement that Mercutio speaks of nothing, and that, I believe, is demonstrably untrue.

There is of course a great deal of divergence of opinion about this scene, and the range of the critics is certainly not measured by Granville-Barker and Schücking. A more recent writer, John Vyvyan, implies that Mercutio is full of hot air, borrowing his terminology from Shakespeare himself. "There is a little more wind," he says, talking about the lines that immediately follow, "and then Benvolio brings the speech to a stop."[5] Wind indeed—however, Vyvyan does not find the speech dramatically inappropriate. It is the fashion these days to explain all of the passages in Shakespeare in terms of dramatic function, and Vyvyan believes that this one contributes to the balanced structure of the play. It stands, he argues rightly, in relation to the feast scene as the conjuration scene (later) stands in relation to the balcony scene.[6] Despite appearances he thinks there is a logical arrangement of speeches in the play, and he implies that it is the job of the critic to discover such relationships. Doubtless he is correct, but the relationship itself does not necessarily mean that the Queen Mab speech is not digressive. To support that argument we must look further.

One assumption that lies behind the contentions of both Granville-Barker and Schücking that the passage is a digression (whether it disturbed the audience or not) is the old argument that we cannot apply the presumptions of Aristotelian criticism to Shakespeare. That conclusion—it has lately taken on an aphoristic flavor—is both right and wrong. It is quite obvious that Shakespeare liked mixed genres, particularly the mixture of chronicle (or history) with tragedy, a mixture that was hardly considered by Renaissance literary critics. Certainly he never wrote the *pure* tragedy that Aristotle had in mind when he wrote his description, using Sophocles for a model. But to say that does not imply that the whole method of Aristotelian analysis is inapplicable to Shakespeare. A play still has parts, a beginning, a middle, and an end; plot and character are still its most essential elements, whether Sophocles or Shakespeare wrote it. That Shakespeare does not lend himself easily to Aristotelian analysis does not prove that he was a "natural genius"—not if that term means that the hand that held the pen let words fly effortlessly, without art, to the page. Ben Jonson started that story for reasons best known to himself, but T. W. Baldwin certainly dispelled it.

The deliberate quality of Shakespeare's craft is perhaps concealed by the fact that he wrote for the living stage. Therefore his texts come down to us in somewhat imperfect form. But doubtless he blotted thousands of lines. There is hardly a critic today who would dare deny his careful artistry; we have studied Shakespeare too closely to adhere to naïve views of earlier centuries. Nevertheless, there are sometimes digressions in the plays and elements that seem sometimes destructive of dramatic unity. But too often that appearance is our fault rather than Shakespeare's. Sometimes we are too quick to assign to an Aristotelian limbo passages that puzzle us but may have been quite clear to people in Shakespeare's day.

I believe the Queen Mab speech is such a passage. Of course if we examine the speech in the light of the Aristotelian dictum that everything in a play must be necessary to the development of the action, and then agree with Vyvyan that the speech is part of a planned parallel structure, we may find ourselves begging the question. We can, however, find evidence to support the argument by examining the rhetorical devices that the speech contains. We can turn to another element of the play, its diction, for the explanation we are seeking.

The Queen Mab speech takes place after Romeo and Mercutio have been engaged in a hot, fast match of wits, the game of Elizabethan bandying that so delighted Shakespeare's audience and often puzzles us. Some critics have badly misinterpreted the meaning of the game in *Romeo and Juliet*. They have even considered Romeo's astuteness at wordplay in the earlier scenes to indicate an insincerity in his feeling for Rosaline, his first mistress in the play. It is true there are plenty of indications by Shakespeare, several in terms of the theme of appearance and reality, to indicate that Romeo's passion for Rosaline was not to be enduring. That sort of passion was to come later when he met Juliet. But Romeo is

always clever at wordplay, both before and after he meets
Juliet. He may occasionally lose the advantage for a moment
or two, but he is capable of besting all his partners except
Juliet herself. With her he may find it somewhat difficult to
concentrate on scoring.

Excepting Juliet, Mercutio is Romeo's most worthy opponent at the game of wit, and the fact that Mercutio is
realistic about love, as well as bawdy, serves to advance the
plot of the play. His suggestion that there are other fish in
the sea indicates a means whereby Romeo may be cured of his
infatuation. The suggestion leads directly to the clandestine
visit to the Capulet ball and the subsequent meeting of the
lovers. At that point Mercutio scores a momentary advantage
at the game. Nevertheless, Romeo finally manages either to
best him or to drive him away from the subject. That, too, is
a sort of victory of words. That is what happens when
Mercutio breaks off the contest and begins the Queen Mab
speech. Pressed too hard by his opponent, he seeks respite
by breaking the train of thought, though he returns to it very
quickly—before the end of the speech, as I shall argue. But
actually it is incorrect to think of many word games played
by Romeo and Mercutio; what they do is play the same one
throughout several scenes with an occasional respite. It is a
little like a chess match carried on at luncheons between two
players that meet every day. The men on the board, in this
case the verbal counters, remain in exactly the positions in
which they were left until the session is resumed. Once we
understand the structure of the game, it is no longer possible
to believe that Shakespeare used wordplay at the beginning to
emphasize the earthy nature of Romeo's passion for Rosaline
in contrast to a more spiritual attraction for Juliet. Shakespeare did not need to do that, for the difference is clear very
early in the play, almost from the instant Romeo and Juliet
see each other.

"Whoever loved that loved not at first sight?" Marlowe asked, concerning Leander's grand passion for Hero. Even Spenser, who seems not to have approved of the idea, was attracted by it; his heroine Britomart fell in love with Artegall on first seeing his image. Spenser was repelled by Marlowe's eroticism, but it fired Shakespeare's imagination. He tried it himself in *Venus and Adonis*, but as C. S. Lewis has suggested he was not quite at home there. In *Romeo and Juliet* he tried again, beginning with love at first sight, though mingling the eroticism with deeper themes. Yet at the start of the play it is quite clear that Romeo's intentions towards Rosaline are what we would call dishonorable. Moreover, his attraction for Juliet was similar. Until she proposed marriage the essential difference between Juliet and Rosaline was simply that Juliet encouraged Romeo while Rosaline resisted him. It was to prevent us from seeing this too clearly that Shakespeare kept Rosaline off stage, though she was a guest at the ball and readily available. After the proposal, which Romeo accepted as quickly as he could draw his breath and assimilate the idea, the course of the loves is quite different.

The wordplay that serves as a setting for the Queen Mab passage is not needed to make that point, which indeed cannot be entirely clear before the balcony scene and the proposal. Actually the speech itself interrupts the game at a moment when Mercutio seems to have a slight advantage, but in this game as at chess one must think ahead, and it is possible that Mercutio cannot see his future gambits. Perhaps Romeo is a little off his mettle at that instant, but, one concludes, Mercutio somehow realized he had gone about as far as he could. Either it was best to quit while he was ahead, or he needed time to think of a new tack.

It may be suggested that the whole Queen Mab speech was a counter in the game of wits. It contains an astonishing number of brilliant rhetorical figures, and the use of tropes and figures was a means of scoring at the game. But I cannot quite believe it, though the game is actually resumed before the speech is concluded. The tone of the passage after Romeo's gambit, "I dreamt a dream tonight" (I.iv.49) is altered. There are only a few more counters before the beginning of the famous apostrophe:

Mercutio: And so did I.
Romeo: Well, what was yours?
Mercutio: That dreamers often lie.
Romeo: In bed asleep, while they do dream things true.

And Mercutio, "O, then, I see Queen Mab hath been with you," and he begins the speech.

One wonders what Romeo's dream might have been, but he never tells us. It is an unwritten assumption in the battle of wits that when one's opponent gets a step ahead by changing the subject to something one cannot follow, then the field must temporarily be relinquished. That Romeo does. The business is very interesting. It appears that Romeo has made a miscalculation. Instead of asking Mercutio about his dream, Romeo should have gone on with his own plan. But for an instant he relaxed his guard, and Mercutio slipped in his rapier. All Romeo can do is rather lamely turn the verb *lie*, but to go much further might drive him into a position he wishes to avoid. It would seem now there is a good chance for Mercutio to destroy him and win the game. He needs only to turn the verb *lie* once more to some disparaging reference to lovers in bed, in his customary bawdy fashion. But the play is full of surprises. Instead of the answer the audience must have anticipated, Mercutio begins the Queen Mab speech.

The key words in this prologue are *dream, lie, bed,* and perhaps *asleep.* Shakespeare has taken pains to construct a situation and then abruptly withdrawn from it. That technique is of course not unusual with him and makes for interesting dialogue. But I think it is important that he uses it here, for the abrupt change of subject causes the Queen Mab speech to stand out in the scene (if most of the critics are right). Why should Shakespeare, unless he were just abominably careless, call our attention so forcefully to something if it turns out to be just window dressing? If the speech is not necessary in the Aristotelian sense, it is certainly deliberate. We are reminded of that again at its end—Shakespeare is almost never careless about important points—by a return to the dream theme. "True, I talk of dreams," Mercutio admits, "Which are the children of an idle brain, / Begot of nothing but vain fantasy, / Which is as thin of substance as the air. . . ." As it draws to a close the whole scene is altered in mood from the gay levity of the word game to a grave portent of dire events to come, as Mercutio turns to the spin of fortune for his theme and Romeo picks up the new tack. It is time, too, for the beginning of *Romeo and Juliet* is as airy as any cape and sword comedy. The time has come to clear the atmosphere and get on with the real play, and in doing so Shakespeare decided to use the Queen Mab speech set between two dream references much as a jeweler sets a precious gem between two chips of diamond.

That the speech is so carefully bound between the twin prongs of dream reference is itself unusual and indicates that Shakespeare was particularly attracted to it, whether or not it was necessary to the dramatic action. But we should not forget that Shakespeare was not writing opera or musical comedy, whatever he permitted in the entr'acte, and the impression he gives over and over again is that he resented intrusions rather than welcomed them.[7] As theatre-goers understand, the plot of musical comedy sometimes suffers from the intrusion of dance and the plot of opera from the formalized singing of arias, but the harm, because the plot usually does not matter much, is balanced by the attractiveness of the digression. We go to musical comedy for the dance as much as for the story. In an unusually good production, the disparate elements can be integrated, as Agnes de Mille, for example, tried to do with the dances in *Oklahoma,* making them rise from the dramatic action and contribute to the development of the story.

Not only has Shakespeare set apart an apparent digression between two dream references, but, as has been often noted, dream references themselves are usually prophetic in Shakespeare. "The testimony of dreams," Sister Miriam Joseph reminds us (though she had in mind a different sort of testimony), "is invariably authenticated by subsequent events."[8] That principle works here, too, for the dream turns prophetic. The device in the rhetoric books is called *ominatio.* But what of the Queen Mab speech itself? Did Shakespeare just dig it out of his notebook or his brain and find he could not resist setting it? Or did he have a dramatic reason? That is the first question, and as a matter of fact the answer should not be difficult, for Shakespeare, as one critic has said, "was not a maker of rag-mats."[9]

Mercutio's Queen Mab speech is both attractive poetry and a masterly accumulation of rhetorical devices. It is necessary to remind ourselves that the two were not inimical in Shakespeare's day. But before examining the devices themselves, let us consider the content they are calculated to emphasize. The speech is a description of the Queen of the Fairies. Its origin in Elizabethan folklore has been disputed;[10] the main ideas are by no means unique in Shakespeare. Jonson has a similar description in his lyric "This Is Mab, the Mistress Fairy" (perhaps dependent on Shakespeare's passage), but he begins by listing her pranks. She "doth nightly rob the dairy," "She that pinches country wenches," etc. He ends with a traditional nuptial preview, absent in Shakespeare:

And on sweet Saint Anne's night
Feed them with a promised sight,
Some of husbands, some of lover,
Which an empty dream discovers.[11]

(For some reason Furness did not mention Jonson's lyric in the *Variorum*.) Mercutio is of course interrupted before he gets that far, and if we wish to find the conclusion we have to search beyond his speech. Jonson's St. Anne is generally taken to be a misprint for St. Agnes, and it is Keats' version of that story that we are likely to remember. But in Jonson's version the powers of Mab are arranged in ascending order, ending with the power to bring to maidens the dream of future husbands or lovers (though perhaps in that order there is a touch of irony). In Mercutio's poem the order is different, and the climax is omitted. That too is a matter of rhetoric, for *ellipsis* was a respectable figure, and if Shakespeare thought of the interruption as constituting *ellipsis* then the figure is magnified far beyond the examples of the rhetoric books. But it is not possible to say for certain that Shakespeare had intended *ellipsis* here, though that was a device he often used. He exaggerated rhetorical figures to such size that they became analogous to extended metaphors. The process itself (though not in the way Shakespeare used it) is fairly typical of Elizabethan poetry; one need only look again at Donne's stiff, twin compasses that encircle the whole poem "A Valediction Forbidding Mourning."

If Shakespeare thought of the interruption to Mercutio's speech as an *ellipsis*, then there is a sort of balance provided between the larger aspects of the poem and the minutiae of the passage. Mercutio begins with an exacting description of the fairy, her whips, her chariot, etc., and as she is a very small fairy to begin with, there is implicit a sort of comparison between the microcosm and the macrocosm. Perhaps that is being too literal, but surely the doctrine of correspondences was never far from Shakespeare's mind.

Mercutio follows with a description of the mischief Queen Mab does:

> And in this state she gallops night by night
> Through lovers' brains, and then they dream on love;
> O'er courtiers knees, that dream in curtsies straight;
> O'er lawyers' fingers, who straight dream on fees;
> O'er ladies lips, who straight on kisses dream . . .

That slight reference to love with which Mercutio ends the above verses is as close as he comes to the traditional nuptial preview. But in a sense the whole of the play up to this point has been preparing for a nuptial preview, the meeting of the lovers, and I should think the audience would be able to supply the unstated parts from their general knowledge of the folklore. The sequence moves from money to kisses (love in a sensual regard), and then Mercutio repeats it, referring again to courtiers and their ambition for high place, to parsons dreaming of another benefice (again money), adding soldiers with their dreams of "cutting foreign throats." Then he returns to love this time with bawdy overtones: "This is the hag, when maids lie on their backs, / That presses them and learns them first to bear, / Making them women of good carriage."

These sensual references, arranged climactically, emphasize both the main love theme of the play and Mercutio's role as a scoffer at love, which he plays only with respect to Rosaline, Romeo's unseen mistress. He is dealing in the real subjects of the play concealed in airy bandying about the Queen of Fairies. The talk of money and place (the ambition of courtiers) stands in relation to the outer world of Verona that threatens the lovers in the action of the play as microcosm to macrocosm, as the talk of love stands in relation to the real love of the play. That Mercutio is bawdy and sensual does not alter the correspondence, for the real love in the play is also sensual. But the correspondence is surely not exact. In the Queen Mab speech Mercutio considers all three —money, place, and love—to be madnesses. The idea of love as a madness is by no means unusual in Elizabethan literature, and Romeo passes through that state with both mistresses as his love becomes refined into *fino amore*.

Actually neither money nor place, though they are both concerns of the outer world apart from love, have anything to do with the major action of the play. Money is never even mentioned. So far as place is concerned Romeo is as acceptable a suitor for Juliet as Paris except for the quarrel between the Montagues and Capulets. The outer world that threatens love is symbolized in the main action of the play entirely by violence, and Shakespeare, when he permits Mercutio a second turn of the wheel, a restatement in the Queen Mab speech, brings in violence directly. The fairy makes soldiers dream of "cutting foreign throats, / Of breaches, ambuscadoes, Spanish blades." A main theme of the play is directly suggested. In fact the reference to Spanish blades suggests dueling and the way Tybalt is to die. And there is also perhaps an element of satire, for Mercutio, himself a violent man, is making fun of violence. One of the most human traits of Shakespeare's characters is their ability to joke at themselves, and Mercutio is no exception to the rule.

The Queen Mab speech, then, presents what were the main reasons for marriage—money, place, and love—and then presents what in the milieu of *Romeo and Juliet* was a principal destructive force—violence. There is really very little else in Mercutio's speech, save only at the beginning the charming description of the Fairy Queen. Mercutio has stuck rigorously to the main subjects of the play, and an audience not wholly carried away by the charm of his poetry should have recognized that the speech emphasizes Shakespeare's themes and even suggests, faintly, the outcome of the action. It seems clear that the Queen Mab speech is no operatic interlude.

We are committed to the belief that the complete, uncut version of a play is always superior, and there is some reason to believe that that is the right opinion to hold of *Romeo and Juliet.* Certainly Shakespeare never intended for the play to be carried entirely by its action; for one thing it is a very wordy play, in its early acts the most rhetorical of the tragedies. And the words, both the rhetoric and the poetry, are carefully arranged to give the effect of an architectural structure. Shakespeare proceeds by a series of delicate balances, which he would probably have called correspondences, to construct an edifice that would by itself excite the admiration of his audience. We cannot afford to forget that admiration, according to Sidney, though not entirely for the structure of the drama, was a legitimate end of tragedy, in addition to the Aristotelian aims of arousing pity and fear.

Shakespeare by no means followed Sidney's dicta slavishly. For example, Sidney would not have approved of his original treatment of tropes and figures. We usually understand Sidney's criterion of admiration to refer to the subject matter of drama, but I have no doubt Shakespeare would have interpreted more liberally. Not only does he require us to admire the subject matter of his tragedies, but he also asks us to admire the structural complexity and the rhetorical brilliance. If we consider closely the diction in the plays, we must conclude that this was a very important matter for the Elizabethan audience to note and admire. Because we in the twentieth century no longer adhere to, or even discuss very often, a doctrine of correspondences, we have lost some of the ability to appreciate the complexities of Shakespeare's structure. And we have also largely lost the ability to admire the rhetorical brilliance of his manipulation of figures. To appreciate these aspects of his work we need to recall that a large portion of Shakespeare's audience, during their school years, concentrated on those two rhetorical questions: *Hic est figura* and *Per quam figura?*[12] And the Queen Mab speech is certainly a demonstration of rhetorical fireworks, the actual figures of which are difficult to pin down because of their complexity.

There are in the speech two extended examples of *anaphora* (that is, initial repetition) coupled with *zeugma* (forcing one verb to serve many clauses):

1- Her waggon-spokes made of long spinners legs;
   The cover, of the wings of grasshoppers;
   Her traces, of the smallest spider web;
   Her collars, of moonshine's wat'ry beams;
   Her whip, of cricket's bone; the lash, of film;
   Her waggoner, a small grey-coated gnat . . .

2- And in this state she gallops night by night
   Through lovers' brains, and then they dream of love;
   O'er courtiers knees . . .
   O'er lawyers' finger . . .
   O'er ladies lips . . .

Both of these figures are brilliantly executed and the first (if we may judge from the pleasure it seems to have accorded the critics) brilliantly conceived. They must have aroused the admiration of Shakespeare's audience. Indeed the audience could hardly have missed them, for they are far better examples than the usual textbook figures provided by Puttenham, Sherry, or Day.

There is no need to document Shakespeare's use of tropes and figures. J. W. Draper has analyzed those used in *Romeo and Juliet*, without specifically mentioning *anaphora* and *zeugma*.[13] It is interesting to note that Mercutio's figures here are not those specially favored by the leading characters in the play. The Queen Mab speech is a solo performance, and possibly Shakespeare chose the figures to indicate some particular attribute of Mercutio's character. By their words Shakespeare's characters are made known to us—sometimes even more than by their actions—and Mercutio's explosion into pyrotechnics in the Queen Mab speech, even disregarding the particular figures he employs, certainly emphasizes his character. Mercutio is, of course, mercurial; that is the humour concealed in the anagram of his name, and that is the way he behaves.

Next to Romeo and Juliet he is the most important person in the play, for it is from his mercurial action in picking a quarrel with Tybalt that the tragedy proceeds. He is the efficient cause. Perhaps it is difficult for a modern audience to forgive him for his headstrong conduct, though we can sometimes overlook it. But Elizabethans surely understood, and partly from the rhetorical performance, that what Mercutio did, bad as it turned out, was completely in character. It was not his fault that he became the agent of Romeo's banishment and eventually the death of the lovers, for he could not change what he was. Mercutio and Tybalt are the two real humour characters in the play, though Romeo and especially Juliet are sometimes dominated by their humours, too. In that sense Shakespeare was frank with us when he said in the prefatory sonnet that the lovers were star-crossed. Moreover, Shakespeare needed to emphasize Mercutio's dominant humour or run the grave risk of permitting his audience to blame Mercutio and thereby draw wrong conclusions about the play. Fate plays its part in *Romeo and Juliet*, though the lovers are not brought to their tragic end because of the blind touch of accident sweeping across their lives. Accident occurs, but they also create their own destiny because of what they are. Through Mercutio, and perhaps Tybalt as well—humour characters—the process was made clear to the Elizabethan audience. We who do not understand the theory of humours that sometimes lay behind the characterization are likely to be puzzled.

The gods do not cast dice for the happiness of Romeo and Juliet, nor are they guilty because of their passions and sentenced to death. In fact death itself is both an ending and perhaps a victory for them; Shakespeare hints that they are to be together for eternity (symbolized by their statues raised in gold). And there is another romantic victory secured by their deaths in that the violence in Verona is brought to an end. They have paid with their lives to better the world they occupied. The theme of love in the play has won over the theme of violence. Their passion, arising from their characters, arranged for it. There is the high taste of *grand amour* about all.[14] To Shakespeare great passion was always forgivable. Sensual in nature, it rises above sensuality, as according to the doctrine of Ficino the lover rises from worship of the lady to worship of the ideal and finally of God. Great passion is an elevating element that helps to raise characters to tragic intensity. Shakespeare was to use parts of the same mechanism in *Antony and Cleopatra*. To bring about all this magic and surpass the ordinary love myth, Shakespeare required a certain kind of agent, a particular Mercutio—on the one hand a bawdy realist and a puncturer of love's ideals and on the other the man of mercurial temperament, a brilliant intellectual to challenge Romeo at wordplay yet a man to start the fatal quarrel with Tybalt, even though he usually appeared to be anything but a brawling man. It was a difficult role to cast, for Mercutio was not to be a mere counterpart for Tybalt attached to the Montague camp. He needed to be a great deal more than that, which Shakespeare emphasizes by insisting on his relationship to the Prince rather than to Romeo. It was no small task to create such a complex character and then kill him off at the beginning of the third act. The sparkling performance of Mercutio in the Queen Mab speech was of course part of the machinery Shakespeare used. Did it work? For us? Granville-Barker says no, that the speech is puzzling, and that it is sometimes altogether cut out of the play. For the Elizabethans? We cannot be certain; there is no testimony. But it is true we hardly recognize the dominant ideas of the period, the doctrine of correspondence or the ladder of love, and we seldom appreciate the tropes and figures familiar to the man of the Renaissance.

It remains to be said that recognition of very striking figures of *anaphora* and *zeugma* in the Queen Mab speech by no means exhausts the possibilities of rhetorical analysis. For instance, there is another, subtler sense in which the entire passage is a figure of rhetoric. We have noted that it comes around in content, full circle to the point where Mercutio is interrupted (a very different arrangement from that Jonson used in his lyric). It stops on a note of sensuality typical of the speaker. Of course Mercutio was cut off, but we should remember Shakespeare was not. Sensuality in Shakespeare, except as a preliminary rung on the ladder of love, seldom leads to a rewarding end. It has been said often enough that Shakespeare was an upholder of middle-class morality, for which there is evidence in this play. Juliet herself may be the most striking example. She was never prepared to surrender without matrimony. Her proposal took Romeo off his guard and left him speechless for a moment, but when he did speak again, after a dialogue between Juliet and the nurse during which he presumably thought over what he must be committed to, he accepted her terms with alacrity. For Shakespeare's treatment of the opposite side of the issue one need seek no further than *Troilus and Cressida*. Illicit passion did not bring Romeo and Juliet to their tragic end, though there are critics who have thought so. Instead the sensual nature of love is necessary to the course of the action and the final fulfillment, and Mercutio's sensuality, especially in this speech where he previews the main themes of the play, resembles the figure *ominatio* (the prognostication of evil) or perhaps *paraenesis* (the warning of impending evil); it is difficult to distinguish the two. There is here a delicate hint of a process Shakespeare employed more directly when he came to deal with the soothsayers in *Julius Caesar* and *Antony and Cleopatra*. But perhaps that is asking more from the Queen Mab speech than is really necessary, for it is clear enough from the content that the speech points forward towards the tragedy that will follow. If *ominatio* or *paraenesis* are operative figures in the passage, they are used to reinforce what has already been said, but this is Shakespeare's method. One might almost conclude that Shakespeare applied literally to the process of play-making Thomas Elyot's admonition to the schoolmaster in *The Governour*, where he insisted that they explicate the figures "leaving nothing . . . undeclared or hid from [the] scholars." Though not always understood or appreciated, Shakespeare's method was to leave as little as possible for the audience to decode.

The main themes of the play, then, run through the Queen Mab speech almost as *leitmotif* to the delicate fairy description, a dramatic necessity because the course of *Romeo and Juliet* was not clear from the beginning, despite a prefatory sonnet. It only becomes clear after the deaths of Mercutio and Tybalt in the third act. Two full acts are spent before the action is directed towards tragedy. Yet *Romeo and Juliet* is not really such a mixture of genres (at least not in an English sense). Rather it is a very unusual play, an inspired modernization of tragedy for the Elizabethan stage, the first great tragedy that did not deal heavily in Senecan elements (such as incest, adultery, rape, and arson). Though the Queen Mab speech actually may have failed for the Elizabethan audience, the likelihood seems quite otherwise.

There is still another rhetorical aspect of the Queen Mab

speech we have not examined, one that does not point directly towards the denouement of the play. The whole speech serves in a sense as the figure *philophronesis* (that is, mitigation by gentler words) as a turn in the word game between Romeo and Mercutio. Compare the bawdy Mercutio of the conjuration scene or the deadly angry one of "A plague on both your houses" with the tassel-gentle, charming apostrophizer of the Fairy Queen. This is the side of Mercutio's character that is nowhere reflected in Tybalt. Would Shakespeare's audience have recognized what he was doing through such figures? It seems clear they understood his meaning, for we do not blame Mercutio for the tragedy that encompassed the lovers.

The Queen Mab speech, then, contains a heavy complex of figures whose use was deliberate. No Elizabethan writer would employ such a heavy load of figures without meaning to focus attention on the speech in question. It is inconceivable that attention could be drawn so forcibly to a passage that was meant to be little more than a charming digression. Once we understand the preoccupation with rhetoric in the speech, we realize that Shakespeare did not work that way. The speech does point forward to the dramatic action, and, secondly, it illustrates the fullness of Mercutio's character, also necessary to the development of the plot. It is a small essential in the complex structure of *Romeo and Juliet*, balanced, as the critic John Vyvyan has shown, by the feast as the conjuration scene (also seemingly extraneous on the surface) is balanced by the balcony scene. But the Queen Mab speech is not there just to furnish a neat balance and correspondence. It explains Mercutio to the audience, and he in turn directs the audience to the action that is to follow. Without such a careful structure *Romeo and Juliet* would, in my opinion, be likely to be a mass of disparate elements, which it certainly is not, and Shakespeare a weaver of rag-mats, which he certainly was not.

CHAPTER FIVE

The Play's The Thing

WHILE THIS ESSAY is primarily concerned with special aspects of the diction of *Romeo and Juliet,* particularly Shakespeare's use of tropes and figures of rhetoric, it will have been seen that the diction does support certain interpretations of the play against others that have been suggested. An examination of the devices of diction in a play like *Romeo and Juliet* leads naturally toward a consistent interpretation of its meaning. They contribute to the meaning of the play especially as they are used to further the development of character, and sometimes plot, though they are also sometimes used for purposes of economy. Contrary to the opinion of some critics, even in a very rhetorical play like this one Shakespeare seldom furnished ornament for its own sake.

It has been said that the play is not entirely successful as tragedy, though a good performance contradicts that contention. Nevertheless, careful students of the play find faults with both the plot and characterization. For example, Romeo and Juliet are both too young and, as has been suggested, perhaps too ordinary for ideal tragic figures. For some critics accident too often seems to intervene in the development of the action. But, when we leave the theatre, we discover that we have experienced to the fullest the cup of tragedy.

Accordingly, it would seem the fundamental question of the play is not whether this is a tragedy arising from the characterization Shakespeare invented or one brought about largely by fortuitous circumstances. The fundamental question of the play, I believe, is really whether the ending is one of frustration or fulfillment, and, depending on how we answer it, whether the play will seem adequately tragic or a partial failure. Moreover, as M. M. Mahood says when he is discussing this point, "this question emerges from the language of the play itself and thus differs from the conventional, superimposed problem: is *Romeo and Juliet* a tragedy of character or fate?"[1]

If the ending is one of fulfillment, as I contend, it must arise primarily from the development of character. One can have tragedy arising through the intervention of some outside force, as in classical drama. But an ending that suggests eternal fulfillment through the compulsions working within two personalities does not make plausible an assertion that the ending is produced by accident. Fulfillment surely suggests planned development. To say so certainly does not mean that we ought to ignore the role of fate in *Romeo and Juliet*, but here fate is moving within the characters. For example, the letter from Friar Laurence to Romeo in Mantua is, one might say, almost fatally delayed, thereby permitting the tragic action to proceed. But it is what Romeo is moved to do, not the delay of the letter, that has a fatal quality. It is not even certain that had he received the letter the outcome would have been altered. We have no idea how well Friar Laurence informed him. In any case the role of these drives from within is not equivalent to that of the gods in classical tragedy.

Critics who have thought the play was a tragedy of fate, though, are not perhaps entirely at fault; Shakespeare himself encouraged that opinion in the prefatory sonnet by calling the lovers "star-crossed." To us that term means fated— arising entirely from outside forces. It has not been suggested that Shakespeare might have been deliberately misleading us a little or even that the term might have a slightly ironic flavor, but if we consider the development of the action we must see the fateful quality that comes not from the stars but from *within* the two lovers. Although the two appear at last to move inexorably toward the tomb, the audience does not gaze awe-stricken and horror-bound, as in some Greek dramas, at a god-determined progression toward death. Even in the sonnet, if we consider the whole line, "A pair of star-crossed lovers take their life," with its *enallage* (the deliberate use of a case, person, gender, number, tense, or mood for another),[2] Shakespeare does not quite indicate that conclusion. Their stars do cross, and Romeo and Juliet fall in love and eventually die. On the surface at least we seem to be hearing that fate will intervene in the course of the love affair. But the sonnet also could mean just that they were destined to meet and fall in love—not destined by the gods to fall in love and accordingly die.

Their love was the cause of their deaths, but the sonnet does not quite say that. It only announces that they *take* their lives, indicating how they were to die, not why. The line does not say they *lose* their lives. If it did the role of fate would be emphasized. It does not even say their lives were *taken* from them, though that would alter the meaning and require further explanation. Shakespeare through his choice of verbs seems deliberately to have altered the fatal aspect, or at least to have constructed an ambiguity. That he did so knowingly is indicated by the device employed, *enallage* (though there will doubtless be readers who account for the phrase *their life* differently). An ambiguity about the inevitability of the outcome of the play, even so early in the prefatory sonnet, is as it should be, for we discover as the play progresses that there is no force greater than the love within them driving Romeo and Juliet to their deaths.

Shakespeare suggests that Romeo and Juliet are perhaps being driven towards their deaths by a romantic love that is fast becoming an all-consuming passion. That is part of a paradox that creates depth in what is after all a fairly simple story. But passion, no matter how strong it becomes, never does consume them; there is always a strong element of rationality to their love.

Though Shakespeare does not completely resolve this paradox for us, there are other ways of considering the matter that may shed some additional light. One may examine, for example, the philosophical concepts used in the play. Shakespeare understood well the medieval view of man as a rung on the hierarchical ladder of the universe. There man's place was determined or ordained by God, but within the limits of his human nature man was allowed to exercise a certain degree of freedom. Perhaps Shakespeare also felt that there is a contradiction inherent in that metaphysic. He must have been aware of even more extravagant, more paradoxical, Renaissance opinions. There is reason to believe that he sometimes leaned in their direction. Pico della Mirandola, for one, contended that man creates his own future through his actions. To the medieval mind man's abilities were limited; it was possible for man to become a saint but never an angel. The Renaissance, without discovering many solutions, questioned all such bounds. Anything seemed possible. It is hardly necessary to demonstrate that Shakespeare was attracted by this idea, for on it he founded the character of Prospero in *The Tempest*, long after he had considered it in *Romeo and Juliet*.

Equally available to the writer of the Renaissance was the Calvinistic view that man's ultimate spiritual course was pre-determined. Such a position is antithetical to the doctrine of free will, but that seldom stopped the Renaissance thinker from considering both, even considering them together.

Lorenzo Valla, for instance, in *De libero arbitrio*, suggested that while man was surely determined he also exercised free will, an enigma whose solution lay beyond the powers of reason. Shakespeare was surely familiar with such doctrines, if not from Valla, directly from Erasmus, or by way of Calvin. This paradox was, perhaps unconsciously, exploited in *Romeo and Juliet*. There instead of emphasizing the inevitability of the action, Shakespeare pitted his attractive young lovers against the hard-bitten adult world of Verona and, if the game was to be worth the candle, gave them at least an outside chance to win happiness. In a sense they might shape their own destinies. But great love, grand passion, if often destructive to lovers' hopes in this world, may bring fulfillment at least in the next. The lovers may also have a part in the resolution of other issues, by bringing, for example, the feuding families to a truce at the end of the play. At the end war had apparently won; the lovers were dead. But in another way war itself was overcome. That is clear even if we do not think of a fulfillment beyond the grave.

There are also other, more complex matters at stake in the play. It might not be inconsistent with Renaissance psychology (or the Platonic theology of Ficino) to view the ending as having arisen from an excess in the appetitive portions of the souls of Romeo and Juliet. Indeed the humours employed in the play sometimes quite strongly create that impression. The play is often very earthy and sensual; the hero and heroine quite often indulge in bawdy language. Romeo in the earlier affair with Rosaline seems as much motivated by pure sexuality as Euphues in *The Anatomy of Wit*. And a little later, his attraction for Juliet, who indicates from the beginning that she will not resist, arises from the same source in his nature. His feelings for Juliet are at first the same as they were for Rosaline, though they are soon to run much deeper. It is Juliet who thinks of marriage and honor, not Romeo. Like the unseen heroine of Guillaume de Lorris in the *Roman de la Rose,* she encourages him as her suitor not simply because she is a well-bred young lady whose *bel accueil* is extended to all her acquaintances, but because Romeo arouses a deep, passionate response in her nature. It is not his name that matters, we are told in the famous passage, but his person. I am afraid we invariably interpret that passage with reference to the feud, meaning that Juliet wished Romeo might cease to be a Montague so that courtship could proceed. But there is a deeper sense to the words that is quite as important. It is not who Romeo is, in terms of the age-old marriage game, but what he is that matters. He is an extremely attractive young man worthy of her passion which has been aroused in spite of the conventions of Veronese society. Nevertheless, Shakespeare did not move from such considerations to the writing of an *exemplum* in which two delightful young persons were punished for an excess of sensuality. If that had been his intention, why trouble to bring up the question of marriage at all? He treated excessive sensuality directly in *Troilus and Cressida,* but *Romeo and Juliet* was not conceived to be that kind of play.

It is possible to argue for an even subtler interpretation of the psychology of the play, that the lovers were punished for permitting their wills to usurp the functions of their reason. The two arguments are closely related. And Juliet is decidedly a girl of strong will; early in the play she made up her mind not to marry Paris no matter what her parents wished. If she could not marry Romeo, then she would die. But Shakespeare's sympathies and those of the audience are certainly with Juliet. Despite the show of independence, her attack on the conventional, she remains throughout the play a very rational girl. In her first scene she tells Romeo, "You kiss by the book." There is a point at which a young girl with a sound head understands that the flirtation has gone far enough. It is not Juliet who is the irrational, headstrong one, but, we see as the play progresses, her father, old Capulet, who assumes one of the least sympathetic roles in Shakespeare. Like Brabantio in *Othello* or, in a lighter vein, like Polonius in *Hamlet*, the heavy father in Shakespeare is usually doomed.

Sensuality, which at one stage seems to detract from the play's tragic quality, is later shown to be a necessary ingredient of grand passion. Shortly, as love becomes great passion, it adds to the characterization. Shakespeare exploited that idea fully in *Antony and Cleopatra*. To Antony, Cleopatra's kiss was worth a battle or a kingdom, even the greatest kingdom the world had known, and to Cleopatra, Antony's love aroused immortal longings. Neither Antony, an old rake, far worse than Shakespeare painted him if we are to believe Plutarch and Cicero, nor Cleopatra, an infamous courtezan, to speak of her kindly, are very appropriate subjects for great tragedy, at least not in an Aristotelian sense, but Shakespeare made them so by the complicated process of refining their language and forcing us to accept as elevating their grand passion. *Romeo and Juliet* in this sense was the proving ground for the later play. Romeo and Juliet are not the prince and princess of Verona, though they are far better people than Antony and Cleopatra. They are really rather ordinary youngsters from good, Veronese households, neither more nor less important than many others one might find at the Capulet ball. They are too young and too attractive to treat with anything less than full sympathy, and had circumstances been different to start with, had their families been at peace and no unforeseen accidents occurred, they might have loved and wed and lived unnoticed happily ever after. Perhaps that was what Shakespeare meant to imply at the beginning of the play by mixing his genres, for the first two acts of *Romeo and Juliet* are romantic comedy. But Romeo and Juliet are raised to tragic stature, magically perhaps, but by the means Shakespeare had to work with at the time. One of these was to persuade his audience that grand passion was indeed an elevating and ennobling emotion. Another was to place in the mouths of the hero and heroine some of the most beautiful and lyrical language ever written. Still another was to emphasize the rationality of the lovers through their mastery of rhetoric. These matters, which have to some extent been examined in the previous chapters, make it difficult for us to believe that Romeo and Juliet were punished for a tragic flaw that arose from an excess of sensuality, an imbalance in the appetitive portions of their souls.

As hard as it is to decide where the ending of the play lies in the spectrum between frustration and fulfillment, the close observer of Shakespeare's technique may find something overt to encourage the possibility of fulfillment. Shakespeare liked to mirror the macrocosm in the microcosm, to utilize to the fullest the doctrine of correspondences at all levels of the play. In fact *Romeo and Juliet* particularly exemplifies this technique elsewhere.[3] The love affair for Romeo and Juliet is certainly fulfilling; the play reaches its apex at the consummation scene. It would be unusual for Shakespeare to contradict the tone of the play at its ending. If that were what he intended, there would be something wrong with the harmonics of correspondence, something so wrong that it would have disturbed an Elizabethan audience, although perhaps not a modern audience brought up on a different literature and serving a different ethic. But this argument cannot prove the case one way or the other; it only suggests that we examine the play thoroughly.

To some extent that has already been done. Some discerning, modern interpretations of the play, based on the *Liebestod* theme, attempt to persuade us that the ending is truly one of fulfillment. Such speculations are attractive and their conclusions generally correct, although the evidence cited sometimes appears inconclusive. The victory of love over death that we think we find in the play, at least in terms of ordinary events, appears to depend not so much on what the lovers say and do on the stage as it does on the erection of gold monuments to their memory by the bereaved parents, after Romeo and Juliet have ceased to exist as characters in the drama. If the intention to immortalize the lovers in gold (surely the statues never appeared on stage) symbolizes the eternal victory of love over death, it comes almost as an afterthought. But of course the primary purpose of the monuments was to signify peace brought about by union of the feuding families; they serve to settle the second theme of the play, that of war and violence, of injustice in the adult world. Consequently Shakespeare arranged the play so that the feud occupies our final attention. It was desirable to dispel the intensity of emotion after the death of the lovers, but he could not have done otherwise. The lovers had to die to bring the warring factions together. But does that really matter? Which theme serves which? The lovers are sacrificed for peace in the greater society of Verona, but the play is essentially a love story, not the story of a disarmament conference. Shakespeare could not have turned the play into comedy by settling the feud in a different manner, for after the death of Tybalt a marriage would hardly be enough to atone for the bloodletting. He might, however, have deemphasized the reconciliation of the families at the end by confining it to a few lines and omitting reference to the statues. But would not that have compromised his intention? It is proper for love, especially tragic love, to bring about peace. There may be a little thematic confusion at the end of the play, but the theatre-goer feels instinctively that the ending is appropriate. There may even be in it a hint of the peace of God that passeth understanding, but Shakespeare was content, I believe, to leave us with the understanding that the play is essentially about love. His aim was truer in *Antony and Cleopatra*, but he did not miss the mark by far in *Romeo and Juliet*.

It is also enlightening to consider *Romeo and Juliet* in terms of an *amour-passion* myth, as Denis de Rougemont has developed it.[4] According to him *Romeo and Juliet* is the most important resuscitation of the *Tristan and Iseult* myth before Wagner, but he acknowledges that not quite all of the elements of grand passion found in the archetype are present in Shakespeare. Useful as this kind of criticism is, it is perhaps just as easy to think of Shakespeare as his own mythmaker, for he has created a peculiarly Shakespearean version of grand passion (dependent very likely on Spenser's *Faerie Queene*) which incorporates such disparate elements as the *hochste Lust* of *Tristan* with the great theme of marriage for love, which occupies a prominent position in *Romeo and Juliet* and in some of the earlier romantic comedies (especially *A Midsummer Night's Dream*), and comes, according to C. S. Lewis,[5] from the great third and fourth books of Spenser's romantic epic.

It is not certain that the combination of these elements Shakespeare invented for *Romeo and Juliet* quite suited him or even that he took such matters as seriously as we do. When he came to examine them again in *Antony and Cleopatra*, he altered the mixture, omitting entirely the concept of marriage for love; in fact he parodied that theme from *Romeo and Juliet* in the relationship between Antony and Octavia. And he added another ingredient that appears only in embryo in *Romeo and Juliet*, the longing for the eternal. Cleopatra combines what Baudelaire was to call *le gout de l'eternal* with *hochste Lust*. Her most famous line is that spoken on the monument when she decides to follow Antony, "I have immortal longings in me." Juliet only faintly suggests such things when she says that if she cannot marry Romeo death must take her maidenhead, or later when she handles the dagger with which she will extinguish her life. The great idea of love reaching upwards towards eternity, so superbly given expression by Dante, has almost been inverted by Shakespeare in *Antony and Cleopatra*. Dante's heroine, Beatrice, is the antithesis of Cleopatra, and there is almost something blasphemous in mentioning the two together. But the point is worth making, for it serves to indicate that Shakespeare, very much unlike Dante, was little interested in formulating an ethic but instead was searching for satisfactory dramatic material.

How does diction lend force to this view of *Romeo and Juliet*?[6] Precisely because so many of the devices of rhetoric that Shakespeare uses serve to emphasize the development of character in the drama. It is important, for instance, to understand Friar Laurence's role in the play, especially as Shakespeare altered his character from the prototype he found in his source. And it is important to understand the sort of play Shakespeare was writing, and an understanding of the friar's role should assist us in making that kind of judgment. It is necessary to realize that Romeo and Juliet retain to a great extent their rationality even in the throes of the greatest passion in English literature. And the devices of rhetoric help to establish these judgments.

It has been suggested the psychology of the play encourages the opinion that Romeo and Juliet suffer from a flaw of excess passion. Certainly they are passionate lovers, but that is not why they are tragic. Their tragedy arises because they are also intellectuals, brought to their dreadful end through the development of their characters as they struggle with a grand emotion. If Shakespeare seemed ambivalent in combining fate and character or with regard to the elements of grand passion, he did manage to leave us a tragedy of grand passion ending with a touch of exaltation. Romeo and Juliet love each other erotically and are willing to surrender the world as they know it for love. The terms of the myth are those de Rougemont suggests, but there is something beyond that, something that is not developed in *Tristan,* a passion of intellectuals that cannot be divorced from reason and spirit. Antony and Cleopatra are different. They are crafty, practical people who have somehow become involved in a passion beyond their control. Because they are the triple pillar of the ancient world and the exotic queen of Egypt, of whom no man can find surfeit, whom even "the holy priests bless when she is riggish," they fall far and tragically. But Romeo and Juliet must rest their claims on their attractiveness as young people and on the great powers of their intellects combined with the higher parts of the soul, powers that are so often demonstrated in the rhetoric of the play. Therein lies their ability to lose their lives and leave us with the suggestion that perhaps by doing so they found them.

Denis de Rougemont lists marriage for love, mystical passion, and impious license as three principal ingredients of eroticism, conceived as an answer to the Christian doctrine forbidding sensuality of any kind. The first two of these are obviously prominent in *Romeo and Juliet,* and perhaps the last is there, too, if we consider secret marriage to be an impious license. Such marriage had been expressly forbidden by the Council of Trent. Juliet is especially filled with mystical passion, almost from the first moment she sees Romeo, but in the balcony scene she retains her rationality. Though transported by love, she remains a miracle of wit and reason—and rhetoric—and though it comes as an afterthought she does not fail to make it clear to Romeo that her intention is strictly marriage. Thus, as Shakespeare refines and idealizes passion, and synthesizes it on the model Spenser left him, the lovers are made great enough for serious tragedy. Sensual attraction becomes *fino amore*. Shakespeare was working with a very daring conception, which goes a long way, I think, towards explaining why *Romeo and Juliet* is such a rhetorical play.

I am not convinced that *Romeo and Juliet* was entirely clear to the Elizabethan audience, but probably it seemed clearer to them than it does to us because they understood much better than we do the devices employed in it. Whether they thought the ending was satisfactory, whether for them the play ended on a note of frustration or fulfillment, we shall never really know. But after all, the best test of the play is the theatre, where it has survived as vital, meaningful repertoire for centuries. I am tempted to suggest Baudelaire's verses as an appropriate epilogue:

> *Noir assassin de la Vie et de l'Art,*
> *Tu ne tueras jamais dans ma memoire*
> *Celle que fut mon plaisir et ma gloire!*

Notes

Quotations from Shakespeare and line numbers are uniformly from *The London Shakespeare*, ed. John Munro (London, 1958).

CHAPTER TWO

[1] Edith Sitwell, *A Notebook on William Shakespeare* (London, 1962), p. 85.

[2] It is generally believed there was a curtain across the inner stage, though the matter has been much disputed.

[3] Kittredge, in the *Complete Works of Shakespeare* (Boston, 1936), p. 568, noted that the term *collar* in this pun as it appears in *I Henry IV*, meant "hangman's noose." Perhaps that idea also occurred to Shakespeare in *Romeo and Juliet*; the servants after all are talking about the feud. See also Helge Kökeritz, *Shakespeare's Pronunciation* (New Haven, 1953), p. 98.

[4] Abraham Fraunce, *The Arcadian Rhetorike* (London, 1584), q.v.

[5] Sister Miriam Joseph, C.S.C., *Shakespeare's Use of the Arts of Language* (New York, 1947), p. 179. She distinguishes between false syllogism and other kinds of fallacious reasoning, distinctions easily exemplified in Shakespeare. But in this case distinction may be a little too subtle; anyhow, as will be seen, Shakespeare commonly mixed figures.

[6] Judith Dundas, "Allegory as a Form of Wit," *Studies in the Renaissance*, XI, 230.

[7] Robert Burton, *The Anatomy of Melancholy*, eds. Floyd Dell and Paul Jordan-Smith (New York, 1927), I.I.2.10. Of course there are other discussions of the faculties of the soul, but in its essence Burton's theory probably represents fairly what Shakespeare knew.

[8] It is fair to add that there is but slight occasion in *Antony and Cleopatra* for Antony to demonstrate his rhetorical powers and much opportunity for him to be a poet.

[9] Fraunce, pp. 3-4. Also quoted by Dundas, p. 231. Wherever he found it, Shakespeare surely absorbed that advice.

[10] See Sigismund's great speech at the closing of the second act (often compared to Hamlet's "To be or not to be" soliloquy).

[11] I do not mean to insist that Shakespeare had Plato's myth of the cave in mind, though it is not impossible.

[12] It is commonly believed Shakespeare knew Sherry, and certainly rhetoric was at the heart of his school lessons. Very likely he had looked into many of the contemporary rhetorics; see T. W. Baldwin, *William Shakspere's Small Latine & Lesse Greeke*, 2 vols. (Urbana, Illinois, 1944).

[13] None of the rhetoricians are very systematic about naming figures nor very complete in their lists.

[14] See Warren Taylor, *Tudor Figures of Rhetoric* (doctoral dissertation, University of Chicago, 1937). A part of this paper was privately published and distributed by the University of Chicago libraries.

[15] The *OED* cites the first English use of *oxymoron* in 1640.

[16] I am not quite prepared to say that Mercutio was easy to dispense with because of the sort of rhetoric he used, though I cannot help thinking that may be part of the matter. And such a bawdy character would hardly be desirable after the play turns to its more serious aspects. There was a great deal more consciousness of style in the Renaissance than we are generally aware. But Shakespeare would hardly have made style his only clue. That was not his method.

[17] This unusual figure also involves *chiasmus*, and it is impossible to tell how Shakespeare thought of it.

[18] The point is emphasized by H. Kökeritz in *Shakespeare's Pronunciation*, p. 57.

[19] See W. Draper, "Patterns of Style in *Romeo and Juliet*," *Studia Neophilologica*, XXI (1948-1949), 195-210.

[20] Draper, p. 210.

CHAPTER THREE

[1] By and large Shakespeare favored the devices Aristotle favored, and those so frequently reflected in the *Rhetorica ad C. Herennium*: metaphor, simile, synecdoche, prosopopoeia, antonomasia, periphrasis, for vividness; antithesis, isocolon, homoioteleuton, anaphora, epistrophe, polysyndeton, asyndeton, for balance and rhythm. Shakespeare was not set against devices of ambiguity as the classical authors had been, and antanaclasis and paronomasia especially appear with great regularity. The situation is nicely summarized by Sister Miriam Joseph, C.S.C., in her book *Shakespeare's Use of the Arts of Language* (New York, 1947), in the chapter "General Theory of Composition."

[2] H. H. Furness, ed., *A New Variorum Edition of Shakespeare, Romeo and Juliet* (New York: Dover, 1963), p. 110.

[3] H. Granville-Barker, *Prefaces to Shakespeare* (Princeton, 1947), II, p. 303.

[4] H. C. Goddard, *The Meaning of Shakespeare* (Chicago, 1951), p. 121.

5 W. B. C. Watkins, *Shakespeare and Spenser* (Princeton, 1950), p. 46. He speaks of "the tolerance of the worldly-wise friar." It seems to me it is exactly because the friar is lacking in worldly wisdom that he proposes such a naïve plan in the first place. A more worldly man would go to the Capulets and argue the matter.

6 *Variorum*, pp. 149-150.

7 Quoted in *Variorum*.

8 Sister Miriam Joseph, p. 179.

9 Sister Miriam Joseph, p. 242.

10 Thomas Wilson, *The Arte of Rhetorique* (1553), ed. G. H. Mair (Oxford, 1909), p. 114.

11 Wilson, p. 184. I have already mentioned *philophrenesis*, not very important here, and two other figures used to placate and console, *paramythia* and *medela* do not seem to have occurred to Shakespeare in this context.

12 Aphorism in the Renaissance could serve many purposes. Lyly uses it to great extent in *Euphues* (esp. *The Anatomy of Wit*) as a mark of his precious style; Cervantes used it after the beginning chapters of *Don Quixote* (when it apparently first occurred to him) to clarify the character of Sancho Panza, whom he decided to make the voice of common sense.

13 Henry Peacham, *The Garden of Eloquence* (London, 1593), p. 73.

CHAPTER FOUR

1 H. Granville-Barker, *Prefaces to Shakespeare* (Princeton, 1947), II, p. 305.

2 Granville-Barker, p. 305n.

3 L. L. Schücking, *Character Problems in Shakespeare's Plays* (London, 1922), p. 97.

4 Schücking, p. 99.

5 John Vyvyan, *Shakespeare and the Rose of Love* (London, 1960), p. 155.

6 T. W. Baldwin, *William Shakspere's Small Latine & Lesse Greeke*, 2 vols. (Urbana, Illinois, 1944).

7 There seems reason to believe Will Kemp found it difficult to resist breaking into dance when the spirit moved him, even though the lines constrained the action. It is possible that that habit had something to do with Armin's entry into the company.

8 Sister Miriam Joseph, C.S.C., *Shakespeare's Use of the Arts of Language* (New York, 1947), p. 94.

9 Vyvyan, p. 142.

10 See *Variorum*. The etymology of the name has also been disputed.

11 Ben Jonson, from "A Particular Entertainment of the Queen and Prince Their Highness at Althorpe, 1603."

12 Baldwin, II, 36.

13 J. W. Draper, "Patterns of Style in *Romeo and Juliet*," *Studia Neophilologica*, XXI (1948-1949), 195-210. As mentioned in the "Introduction,"

Draper does not examine each of the figures separately but rather provides percentages by types.

[14] *Grand Amour* but not exactly in the *Tristan and Iseult* sense. See "Introduction" and "The Play's the Thing," and then Denis de Rougemont, *Passion and Society* (London, 1956), for a full explanation.

CHAPTER FIVE

[1] M. M. Mahood, *Shakespeare's Wordplay* (London, 1957), p. 57.

[2] Wilhelm Franz, *Die Sprache Shakespeares in Vers und Prosa* (Halle, 1939), does state that requirements of rhyme and metre sometimes account for such grammatical inconsistencies (e.g. Sec. 155, p. 157), but there are other explanations. *Enallage* here might have resulted from ignorance (hardly likely), or from the state of flux the language then endured, or deliberately as a clue to the listener not to take such statements entirely at their face value but rather to puzzle about them.

[3] I have discussed this matter at some length elsewhere in this book and in an essay, *"Romeo and Juliet,* II.i.13: Further Commentary," *Neuphilologische Mitteilungen,* 4 LXIV (1963), 390-400.

[4] See Denis de Rougemont, *Passion and Society* (London, 1956) and *Comme Toi-Meme* (Paris, 1961).

[5] See C. S. Lewis, *Allegory of Love* (Oxford, 1936).

[6] Ernst Robert Curtius, *European Literature and the Latin Middle Ages* (New York: Harper Torchbook edition, 1963), 333, says "the technique of writing perform[s] a dramatic function . . . only in two plays," and he does not include *Romeo and Juliet.* He has not, however, undertaken any sort of close examination of the figures in that play.

Index

Figures, Schemes, and Tropes

General